Castles In Argyll And Bute, including: Inveraray Castle, Kilchurn Castle, Duart Castle, Castle Stalker, Dunollie Castle, Kilmory Castle, Gylen Castle, Dunstaffnage Castle, Duntrune Castle, Dunans Castle, Carnasserie Castle, Skipness Castle, Claig Castle

Hephaestus Books

Contents

Articles

References

Inveraray Castle

Inveraray Castle

External links

- Website for Inveraray Castle [1]
- Its page in the Gazetteer for Scotland [2]

Geographical coordinates: 56°14′15″N 5°04′24″W

Painting of Inverary Castle, 1880

Inveraray Castle, 2006

Kilchurn Castle

Kilchurn Castle

Kilchurn Castle is a ruined 15th century structure on the northeastern end of Loch Awe, in Argyll and Bute, Scotland.

It was the ancestral home of the Campbells of Glenorchy, who later became the Earls of Breadalbane also known as the Breadalbane family branch, of the Clan Campbell. The earliest construction on the castle was the towerhouse and Laich Hall (looks onto Loch Awe). Today, its picturesque setting and romantic state of decay make it one of the most photographed structures in Scotland.

Kilchurn Castle, as seen from boat, 2004

History

Kilchurn Castle was built in about 1450 by Sir Colin Campbell, first Lord of Glenorchy, as a five storey tower house with a courtyard defended by an outer wall. By about 1500 an additional range and a hall had been added to the south side of the castle. Further buildings went up during the 16th and 17th centuries. Kilchurn was on a small island in Loch Awe scarcely larger than the castle itself, although it is now connected to the mainland as the water level was altered in 1817. The castle would have been accessed via an underwater or low lying causeway.

At the turn of the 16th century Kilchurn Castle was extended by Sir Duncan Campbell with the addition of a single storey dining hall built along the inside of the south curtain. During the second half of the century, another Sir Colin Campbell, the 6th Laird, continued to improve the castle's accommodation by adding some chambers to the north of the tower house, and remodelling the parapet. This included the introduction of the circular corner turrets adorned by corbels, most of which have survived remarkably well.

Towards the end of the 16th century the Clan MacGregor of Glenstrae were occupying the castle. Once owning the lands of Glenorchy during the 14th century, until they passed through marriage to the Campbells, the MacGregors were appointed keepers to Kilchurn Castle as the Campbells spent much of their time at Fincharn. This arrangement lasted until the very early part of the 17th century, when a violent feud between the two families brought it to an end and the Campbells retook possession.

In 1681 Sir John Campbell of Glenorchy was made 1st Earl of Breadalbane. To take advantage of the turbulence of the times, he converted Kilchurn into a modern barracks, capable of housing 200 troops. His main addition was the three storey L-shaped block along the north side.

Kilchurn was then used as a Government garrison during the 1715 and 1745 Jacobite risings. The Campbells attempted, unsuccessfully, to sell Kilchurn to the government, after they moved in 1740 to Taymouth Castle in Perthshire.

In 1760 the castle was badly damaged by lightning and was completely abandoned; the remains of a turret of a tower, still resting upside-down in the centre of the courtyard, attest to the violence of the storm.

Engraving of Kilchurch Castle by William Miller, 1846

William Turner's watercolour *Midday* depicts the castle amidst the weather conditions and the geology of Scotland. It was created in 1802.

The ruin is currently in the care of Historic Scotland, and is open to the public during the summer. Access, during summer only, is by either by boat from Lochawe pier, or on foot from Dalmally. Both points are on the A85 road. During 2006 and 2007 there was an access problem to the castle. Network Rail, in accordance with their policy of blocking foot crossings on railway lines, closed the crossing to Kilchurn, effectively removing land access. However in 2007 access via the nearby viaduct was created, restoring landward access once more.

External links

- Kilchurn Castle - Undiscovered Scotland [1]
- Kilchurn Castle - site information from Historic Scotland [2]
- 16th century map of Loch Awe and Kilchurn Castle [3]

Geographical coordinates: 56°24′13″N 5°01′44″W

Duart Castle

Duart Castle

Duart Castle, Isle of Mull

Duart Castle

Clan Maclean \ Maclaine
Branches
Maclean of Duart · Maclean of Coll · Maclean of Ardgour
Lands
Ardgour · Coll ·
Castles
Duart Castle · Glensanda Castle
Septs
Beath · Beaton · Black · Garvie · Lean · MacBeath · MacBheath · MacBeth · MacEachan · Macilduy · MacLaine · McLean · MacLergain · Maclergan · MacRankin · MacVeagh · MacVey · Rankin

Duart Castle or **Caisteal Dhubhairt** in Scottish Gaelic is a castle on the Isle of Mull, off the west coast of Scotland, within the council area of Argyll and Bute. The castle dates back to the 13th century and was the seat of Clan MacLean.

History

In 1350 Lachlan Lubanach Maclean of Duart, the 5th Clan Chief, married Mary, daughter of the John of Islay, Lord of the Isles and she was given Duart as her dowry.

In 1647, Duart Castle was attacked and laid siege to by the Argyll government troops of Clan Campbell, but they were defeated and driven off by the Royalist troops of Clan MacLean.

In September 1653, a Cromwellian task force of six ships anchored off the castle, but the Macleans had already fled to Tiree. A storm blew up on the 13 September and three ships were lost, including *HMS Swan*.

In 1678, Archibald Campbell, 9th Earl of Argyll, son of the Marquess of Argyll, successfully invaded the Clan MacLean lands on the Isle of Mull and Sir John Maclean, 4th Baronet fled the castle and withdrew to Cairnbulg Castle, and afterward to Kintail under the protection of the Earl of Seaforth.

In 1691 Duart Castle was surrendered by Sir John Maclean, 4th Baronet to Argyll. The Campbell clan kept a garrison there, but soon after the that defeat, the Campbells also demolished the stone house of Torloisk, and after loading the furnishings, the door and window sills, joists and slates from the house aboard a galley, they carried away their loot. The stones from the walls they scattered over the moor. Donald Maclean, 5th Laird of Torloisk used some of the stones to build a cottage for his family close to the site of the castle from some of these stones.

In 1751 the castle was abandoned.

Descendants of Archibald Campbell, 1st Duke of Argyll sold the castle in 1801, to MacQuarrie, who in turn parted with it to Campbell of Fossil, who later on sold it to A. C. Guthrie in 1865, and on September 11, 1911, the castle was bought by Sir Fitzroy Donald Maclean, the 26th Chief of the Clan MacLean and restored.

Trivia

The castle was used as a location in the 1999 film *Entrapment*, starring Sean Connery (who has MacLean ancestry on his mother's side) and Catherine Zeta-Jones. The castle also features prominently in the 1971 film *When Eight Bells Toll*, starring Anthony Hopkins.

It is also the setting for the base of Buffy Summers in the first half of *Buffy the Vampire Slayer Season Eight*.

External links

- Official website [1]
- Dark Isle Photos [2]
- 360° image outside the castle [3]
- History of Duart Castle [4]

Geographical coordinates: 56°27′19.55″N 5°39′14.25″W

Castle Stalker

Castle Stalker

Castle Stalker

History

The original castle was a small fort, built around 1320 by Clan MacDougall who were then Lords of Lorn. Around 1388 the Stewarts took over the Lordship of Lorn, and it is believed that they built the castle in its present form around the 1440s. The Stewart's relative King James IV of Scotland visited the castle, and a drunken bet around 1620 resultied in the castle passing to Clan Campbell. After changing hands between these clans a couple of times the Campbells finally abandoned the castle around 1840, when it lost its roof. Then in 1908 a Stewart bought the castle and carried out basic conservation work, and in 1965 Lt. Col. D. R. Stewart Allward acquired the castle and over about ten years fully restored it. Castle Stalker remains in private ownership and is not generally open to the public, although visits can be made by appointment.

Monty Python and the Holy Grail

While most castle scenes in the popular movie *Monty Python and the Holy Grail* (1975) were filmed in and around Doune Castle, Castle Stalker appears in the final scene as "Castle Aaaaarrrrrrgggghhh". First we see the castle from a distance, next John Cleese uses his outrageous French accent to taunt Arthur from its battlements, then finally a massive attack is launched at the castle with an odd conclusion: the police officers who were investigating the death of the historian earlier in the film arrive and arrest Arthur and the other knights. One of them then turns to the camera and says, "All right, sonny, that's enough, just pack that in.", forcibly ending the movie.

External links

- Castle Stalker web site [1]
- Port Appin on Undiscovered Scotland [2]

Geographical coordinates: 56°34′16″N 5°23′10″W

Dunollie Castle

Dunollie Castle

Dunollie Castle (Scottish Gaelic: Dùn Ollaigh) is a small ruin located on a hill north of the town of Oban, on the west coast Scotland. It commands a view of the town, harbour and, outlying isles. The ruin is accessible by a short, steep path. There is no entrance fee, there is a small layby at the foot of the hill. With enough space to park two cars, care must be taken because the layby is on a busy road.

There was a fortification on this high promontory in the days of the kingdom of Dál Riata which was the royal centre of the Cenél Loairn.

Ewan MacDougall, the third chief of the MacDougalls, probably built a castle there in the 13th century. The existing castle ruins date from the 15th century.

Dunollie castle

The MacDougalls, the Lords of Lorne, were direct descendants of Somerled, Lord of the Isles, at a time when the Western Isles were part of Norway. Dougall, Somerled's son held most of Argyll and also the islands of Mull, Lismore, Jura, Tiree, Coll and many others in the 12th century.

The MacDougalls lost the land after siding with MacDougall kinsmen, the Comyns, and fighting against Robert the Bruce. John Stewart of Lorne returned the estates to the clan.

The Marquis of Argyll captured the castle in 1644, but it was returned to the MacDougalls in 1661. In 1746, the MacDougalls abandoned Dunollie Castle and built Dunollie House just downhill from the castle ruins.

In recent years, descendants and members of Clan MacDougall have been encouraged by clan leadership to support local tourism and pay visits to Dunollie, as an ancestral site and important cultural location.

See also

- Royalist rising of 1651 to 1654
- Dunstaffnage Castle

External links

Geographical coordinates: 56°25′35″N 5°29′5″W

Kilmory Castle

Kilmory Castle

Kilmory Castle, also known as **Kilmory House**, is a large 19th century house located just to the south of Lochgilphead, in Argyll and Bute, on the west coast of Scotland. It is currently occupied by the headquarters of Argyll and Bute Council. The gardens are open to the public and form part of a country park on the former estate.

There was a church at Kilmory in ancient times, and in the 1550s the church and lands of Kilmory were held by the Abbot of Paisley. In 1575 the estate was owned by Donald Campbell

Kilmory Castle seen from the south-west.

of Kilmory, and remained in the Campbell family for over 250 years. A house may have stood here as early as the 14th century. The Campbells built a house, or extended the existing one, in 1816-20.

Eliza Campbell, the eldest daughter and co-heir of Peter Campbell, married Sir John Orde, 2nd Baronet in 1824. He inherited the estates following the deaths of his father in law in 1828 and of his wife in 1829. Orde demolished the modest old Campbell house and replaced it with a grand Gothic style mansion designed by architect Joseph Gordon Davis. The core of the older house was retained, but was extended into an L-plan, with new exterior and interior decoration, and a large octagonal tower at the south-west corner. Orde also greatly expanded and improved the grounds and estate, engaging William Hooker to extend the gardens in 1830. Further extensions were carried out in the 1860s.

Location of Kilmory Castle, at NR869867

Orde was buried in the private burial ground adjacent to the house in 1878. His son succeeded to the baronetcy, and changed his name to Campbell-Orde in 1880. The Campbell-Orde Baronets retained the estate until 1938. It passed through several owners thereafter, and served variously as a hotel, hostel and conference centre.

In 1974, Argyll County Council purchased the house to serve as a headquarters for Argyll and Bute District Council, which was formed in 1975. In 1995 local government was reorganised again, although Kilmory remained in use as the headquarters of the new Argyll and Bute unitary authority. An office block extension was built onto the house in 1980-82, to increase the provision of space. Fire damaged the main house the following year, and many interiors had to be refurbished.

The castle is said to be haunted by the ghost of a 'Green Lady'.

References

- Coventry, Martin *The Castles of Scotland (3rd Edition)*, Goblinshead, 2001
- Walker, Frank Arneil *The Buildings of Scotland: Argyll and Bute*, Penguin, 2000

External links

- Argyll and Bute Council: History of Kilmory [1]
- Gardens of Argyll: Kilmory Woodland Park [2]

Geographical coordinates: 56°01′32″N 5°25′17″W

Gylen Castle

Gylen Castle

Gylen Castle, on the southern part of the island of Kerrera in Argyll and Bute, juts dramatically into the sky on the tip of a promontory overlooking the Firth of Lorne.

History

Built in 1582 by the Clan MacDougall. Gylen was only occupied for a relatively short period of time. The castle was besieged then burned by the Covenanters under General Leslie in 1647 during the Wars of the Three Kingdoms.

In May 2006 a restoration of the castle was completed with a £300,000 grant by Historic Scotland and £200,000 raised by worldwide members of Clan MacDougall.

External links

- Map location
- Kerrera on undiscoveredscotland.co.uk [1]

Geographical coordinates: 56°22′47″N 5°33′24″W

Dunstaffnage Castle

Dunstaffnage Castle

Dunstaffnage Castle	
Near Dunbeg, Argyll and Bute, Scotland NM882344	
 Dunstaffnage Castle seen from the east, with the gatehouse in the centre.	
 Shown within Scotland	
Type	Castle of enceinte
Coordinates	56°27′17″N 5°26′13″W
Built	c. 1220s
Built by	Duncan MacDougall of Lorn
Construction materials	Local stone, sandstone

In use	13th century to 19th century
Current condition	Partially ruined
Current owner	Historic Scotland
Open to the public	Yes
Controlled by	Clan MacDougall 13th century to 1309 Scottish Crown 1309 to c.1470 Clan Campbell c.1470 to present

Dunstaffnage Castle is a partially ruined castle in Argyll and Bute, western Scotland. It lies 3 miles (4.8 km) N.N.E. of Oban, situated on a platform of conglomerate rock on a promontory at the south-west of the entrance to Loch Etive, and is surrounded on three sides by the sea.

The castle dates back to the 13th century, making it one of Scotland's oldest stone castles, in a local group which includes Castle Sween and Castle Tioram. Guarding a strategic location, it was built by the MacDougall lords of Lorn, and has been held since the 15th century by the Clan Campbell. To this day there is a hereditary Captain of Dunstaffnage, although they no longer reside at the castle. Dunstaffnage is maintained by Historic Scotland, and is open to the public, although the 16th century gatehouse is retained as the private property of the Captain. The prefix *dun* in the name means "fort" in Gaelic, while the rest of the name derives from Norse *stafr-nis*, "headland of the staff".

History

Before Dunstaffnage

Before the construction of the castle, Dunstaffnage may have been the location of a Dál Riatan stronghold, known as Dun Monaidh, as early as the 7th century. It was recorded, by John Monipennie in 1612, that the Stone of Destiny was kept here after being brought from Ireland, and before it was moved to Scone Palace in 843. However, Iona and Dunadd are both considered more likely, given their known connections with Dál Riatan kings.

The MacDougalls

The castle itself was built in the second quarter of the 13th century, as the seat of Duncan MacDougall, Lord of Lorn and grandson of Somerled. Duncan was unsuccessfully attacked by his Norwegian-backed brother, Uspak, who later died in an attack on Rothesay Castle with Norse forces in the 1230s. He had also travelled to Rome in 1237, and was the founder of nearby Ardchattan Priory. Duncan's son Ewen MacDougall inherited his father's title in the 1240s, and expanded the MacDougall influence, styling himself "King of the Isles". It is probable that Ewen built the three round towers onto the castle, and constructed and enlarged the hall inside.

Following Alexander III's repulse of the Norse influence in Argyll, the MacDougalls backed the Scottish monarchy, and Ewen's son Alexander was made the first sherriff of Argyll in 1293. However, they supported the Balliol side during the Wars of Scottish Independence which broke out a few years later. Balliol's opponent, Robert Bruce, defeated the Clan MacDougall at the Battle of the Pass of Brander in 1308 or 1309, and after a brief siege, took control of Dunstaffnage Castle.

Royal fortress

Now a Crown property, Dunstaffnage was controlled by a series of keepers. James I seized the castle in 1431, following the Battle of Inverlochy, as his enemies were hiding inside. In 1455 James Douglas, 9th Earl of Douglas stayed at Dunstaffnage, on his way to treat with John MacDonald, Lord of the Isles. This followed James II's attack on Douglas power, and led to the signing of the Treaty of Westminster-Ardtornish. A later keeper, John Stewart of Lorn, was a rival of Alan MacDougall, and was stabbed by his supporters on his way to his marriage at Dunstaffnage Chapel in 1463, although he survived long enough to make his vows. Although MacDougall took the castle, he was ousted by James III, who granted Dunstaffnage to Colin Campbell, 1st Earl of Argyll in 1470.

The south facade of Dunstaffnage Castle.

Clan Campbell

The Earls of Argyll appointed Captains to oversee Dunstaffnage, and keep it in readiness, on their behalf. Changes were made to the buildings, particularly the gatehouse, which was rebuilt around this time. The Campbells were loyal allies of the royal house, and Dunstaffnage was used as a base for government expeditions against the MacDonald Lords of the Isles, among others, during the 15th and 16th centuries. James IV visited Dunstaffnage on two occasions.

Dunstaffnage saw action during the Civil War, holding out against Montrose's army in 1644. The castle was burned by royalist troops, following the failure of the rising of the 9th Earl of Argyll in 1685, against the Catholic James VII. During the Jacobite risings of 1715 and 1745, the castle was occupied by government troops. Flora MacDonald, who helped Bonnie Prince Charlie to escape from Scotland, was briefly imprisoned here while *en route* to imprisonment in London.

Decline and restoration

The Campbells continued to add to the castle, building a new house over the old west range in 1725. However, the rest of the castle was already decaying. In 1810 an accidental fire gutted the castle, and the Captains ceased to live here, moving to Dunstaffnage House, some 2 km to the south-east, until this too burned down in 1940. A tenant lived in the 1725 house within the castle until 1888.

Restoration work was undertaken in 1903 by the Duke of Argyll, the castle's owner. This was followed in 1912 by a court case, in which the Court of Session ruled that Angus Campbell, the 20th hereditary Captain, had right of residence notwithstanding the Duke of Argyll's ownership. Works were delayed by World War I, and the planned total restoration was never completed. In 1958, the 21st Captain and the Duke agreed to hand the castle into state care, and it remains a Historic Scotland property. Both the castle and chapel are category A listed buildings and Scheduled Ancient Monuments.

Description

Walls

Dunstaffnage is an irregular quadrangular structure of great strength, with rounded towers at three of the angles. It measures approximately 35 by 30 metres (115 by 98 ft), and has a circumference of about 120 metres (390 ft). The walls are of coursed rubble, with sandstone dressings, and stand up to 18m (60 ft) high, including the

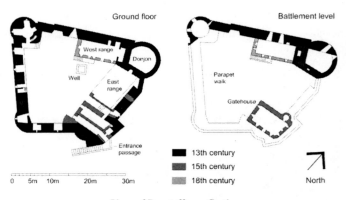

Plans of Dunstaffnage Castle

conglomerate bedrock platform. The walls are up to 3m (10 ft) thick, affording strong defense to this highly strategic location, guarding the entrance to Loch Etive and the Pass of Brander beyond, and today commanding a splendid view. The parapet walk, which once followed the whole of the walls, has been partially restored with new stone flags. The original parapet is now also gone. Arrow slits, later converted into gunloops, are the only openings. Brass cannon recovered from wrecked vessels of the Spanish Armada were once mounted on the walls.

Round towers

Soon after the construction of the castle walls, three round towers were built on the north, east, and west towers. The north tower, or donjon, is the largest, comprising three or four storeys originally, and probably housed the lord's private apartments. The west tower is almost internal, barely projecting beyond the rounded corner of the curtain wall, and could only be entered via the parapet walk. The basement level contains a pit prison which was accessed from above. The east tower was almost completely rebuilt in the late 15th century as a gatehouse. Each tower was probably once topped by a conical roof.

The gatehouse, with the remains of the north-east hall range to the left.

The gatehouse

The gatehouse was built by the Campbells in the late 15th century, replacing an earlier round tower in the east corner. It takes the form of a four-storey harled tower house, with the entrance passage running through half the vaulted basement, the other half forming guard rooms with arrow slits facing the gate. The present approach to the gate is by a stone stair, replacing an earlier drawbridge. The tower was remodelled in the 18th century to provide reception rooms and a private suite. The dormer windows at the top are capped by the pediments from the 1725 house (see below), and bear the date, the Campbell arms, and the initials AEC and DLC, for Aeneas Campbell, 11th Captain, and his wife Dame Lilias. The pediments were moved here during the 1903 restoration works.

Internal ranges

The east range was located between the north and east towers, although only foundations remain. This was the principal range of buildings and contained a large hall above vaulted cellars. The hall had double-lancet windows, decorated with carved patterns, which were later blocked up; their outlines can be seen in the east curtain wall.

A second range stood along the north-west wall, and would have been connected to the hall range by the donjon tower. The ground floor housed a kitchen. In 1725 the range was remodelled into

The north-west range of 1725, with the gatehouse on the right, seen from the parapet walk.

a two-storey house, accessed via a stone stair, and topped with the dormer windows which now form part of the gatehouse. The well in front is original, although the large stone surround is of 19th century date.

East end of Dunstaffnage Chapel, showing the lancet windows and the Campbell burial aisle beyond.

Dunstaffnage Chapel

A ruined 13th century chapel lies around 150 metres (490 ft) to the south-west of the castle. This was also built by Duncan MacDougall of Lorn, as a private chapel, and features detailed stonework of outstanding quality. The chapel is 20 by 6 metres (66 by 20 ft), and formerly had a timber roof. The lancet windows carry dog-tooth carving, and have fine wide-splayed arches internally. The chapel was already ruinous in 1740, when a burial aisle was built on to the east end, to serve as a resting place for the Captains of Dunstaffnage and their families.

Captain of Dunstaffnage

Traditionally, an officer called the Hereditary Captain of Dunstaffnage is responsible for the castle and its defense. The office still exists, and in order to retain the title (now rather a sinecure without military significance), the incumbent is required to spend three nights a year in the castle. No other responsibilities or privileges now attach to the post.

A ghost, known as the "Ell-maid of Dunstaffnage", is said to haunt the castle. A type of gruagach, the ghost's appearances are said to be associated with events in the lives of the hereditary keepers.

References

- Coventry, Martin. *The Castles of Scotland (3rd Edition)*, Goblinshead, 2001
- Grove, Doreen. *Dunstaffnage Castle & Chapel*, Historic Scotland, 2004
- Lindsay, Maurice. *The Castles of Scotland*, Constable & Co. 1986
- Tabraham, Chris. *Scotland's Castles*, BT Batsford/Historic Scotland, 1997
- Walker, Frank Arneil. *The Buildings of Scotland: Argyll and Bute*, Penguin, 2000
- *Encyclopædia Britannica*, Eleventh Edition, 1911

- Historic Scotland Listed Building Report: Dunstaffnage Castle [1], accessed 10 May 2007.
- Historic Scotland Listed Building Report: Dunstaffnage Chapel [2], accessed 10 May 2007.
- National Monuments Record of Scotland Site Reference NM83SE 2, Dunstaffnage Castle[3], accessed 10 May 2007.
- National Monuments Record of Scotland Site Reference NM83SE 3, Dunstaffnage Chapel[4], accessed 10 May 2007.

External links

- Dunstaffnage Castle - site information from Historic Scotland [5]
- RCAHMS Images On-line [6], Dunstaffnage Castle, including plans, aerial views and historical photos.
- RCAHMS Images On-line [7], Dunstaffnage Chapel.
- Dunstaffnage Castle on Undiscovered Scotland [8]

Duntrune Castle

Duntrune Castle

History

It was originally built by the MacDougall clan in the 12th century, along with several other castles in the area, including the MacDougall stronghold of Dunollie Castle near Oban. Duntrune Castle was eventually taken by the Clan Campbell. In 1644, the castle was besieged by the rival MacDonalds, under Alasdair Mac Colla. The Campbells sold Duntrune in 1792, to the Malcolms of Poltalloch. The castle is now owned by Robin Neill Malcolm, current clan chief of the Clan Malcolm.

Duntrune Castle from the east

The curtain wall of the castle dates from the 13th century, although the tower house which forms the main part of the castle is of the 17th century. The castle was renovated in 1954.

Location of Duntrune Castle at
NR793955

The Piper Of Duntrune

The ghost of a handless piper is said to haunt the castle. According to one story, the Macdonald piper was sent into the castle as a spy, but was found out. He was imprisoned, but played his pipes to warn the Macdonalds that their 'surprise' attack was now expected. Alasdair Mac Colla ("Colkitto") retreated, and the piper's hands were cut off by the Campbells.

According to another story, the Macdonalds captured the castle. The Macdonald chieftain needed to return home for some reason and left a small garrison to defend the castle, with the chieftain's personal piper among them. While he was away, the castle was recaptured by the Campbells and the Campbells laid a trap for the Macdonalds.

As the Macdonalds sailed returning to the castle, they heard, as expected the piper playing a tune of welcome from the castle ramparts. As the MacDonald boat grew closer, the Macdonalds were able to discern the tune and recognised it as a warning. The small boat was turned away and the trap failed. To punish the piper, his hands were cut off so that he may never play again. The piper died of his injuries.

During a set of renovations at the castle, workers unearthed a handless human skeleton, whose hands had been removed by clean cuts to the wrist. There is some possibility that this skeleton is that of the Piper Of Duntrune. The skeleton was unearthed and had been buried near the castle. There was evidence of an Episcopalian burial, although as a MacDonald the Piper would most likely have been Catholic.

See also

- Duntroon, Australian Capital Territory, a location named after the castle
- Robert Campbell (1769–1846), descended from the Campbells of Duntroon

External links

- Gazetteer for Scotland [1]

Geographical coordinates: 56°06′04″N 5°33′01″W

Dunans Castle

Dunans Castle

Dunans Castle is an historic structure located in Glendaruel, in the Argyll and Bute region of Scotland. Shown on maps in 1590, the building was elaborated into a castle in 1860, the castle sits on 16 acres (65000 m^2) of ground and in 2001, was ruined by fire.

History

The castle was originally home to the Fletcher Clan who moved to the site c.1745 carrying with them the door of their previous home at Achallader Castle. The original mansion-style

Dunans Castle viewed from the road

house (to the left in the picture) was converted into its present dramatic Franco-baronial form by the architect Andrew Kerr and consisted of four main apartments and 6 bedrooms. The building passed out of Fletcher hands in 1997. The B-listed castle was gutted by fire on 14 January 2001 while being run as a hotel and the building was left as a ruin. Now under new ownership, the site, including a Victorian path network, is undergoing an extensive program of restoration aided by the Scottish Laird project and the Dunans Charitable Trust.

Bridge & Mausoleum

Bridge leading from the main road to the castle

Dunans Bridge is an A-listed structure, designed by Thomas Telford in 1815 and constructed to commemorate the battle of Waterloo. The three-arched rubble construction is considered internationally important as it is the only extant bridge of this type. It stands over 15 metres from the river bed and has been voted one of Scotland's ten best bridges.

Associated with the site, but still in the ownership of the Fletchers is the Fletcher Mausoleum, a grade C listed structure.

The Stronardron Douglas Fir

Also associated with the site is the tallest tree in the UK, the Stronardron Douglas Fir. This tree, standing at 63.79 metres was originally planted by Archibald Fletcher in 1848-9 as part of a stand intended to frame views to and from Dunans Castle.

External links

- Dunans Heritage Project [1]

Geographical coordinates: 56°4′21″N 5°8′58″W

Carnasserie Castle

Carnasserie Castle

Carnasserie Castle (also spelled **Carnassarie**) is a ruined 16th century tower house, noted for its unusual plan and renaissance detailing. It is located around 2km to the north of Kilmartin, in Argyll and Bute, western Scotland, at grid reference NM837009.

The approach to Carnasserie Castle from the south-east.

History

The castle was built by reforming churchman John Carswell, who was Rector of Kilmartin, Chancellor of the Chapel Royal at Stirling, and later titular Bishop of the Isles. Carswell published the first book to be printed in Scottish Gaelic, a translation of John Knox's *Book of Common Order*. Construction began in 1565 using masons brought from Stirling. Although the castle was notionally built for Carswell's patron, the Earl of Argyll, he intended it as a personal residence for himself.

On Carswell's death in 1572, the castle passed to his patron, the Earl of Argyll. Later, in 1643, the 8th Earl of Argyll sold Carnasserie to Sir Dugald Campbell, 3rd Baronet of Auchinbreck. Following the 9th Earl's failed uprising in support of the Monmouth Rebellion, against James VII in 1685, the castle was blown up by Royalist forces. Although the outer walls remain largely undamaged, the ruins were never repaired. In the 19th century the estate was sold to the Malcolms of Poltalloch, who also own nearby Duntrune Castle. Today it is a Scheduled Ancient Monument in the care of Historic Scotland (no entrance fee; open in summer).

Architecture

Carnasserie Castle seen from the south-west, with the hall house in the foreground.

Carnasserie has only ever been slightly altered, in the late 17th century, and so presents an accurate picture of 16th century architecture. Although sited on raised ground close to a strategic pass at the head of Kilmartin Glen, it was designed more for domestic rather than military purposes.

The castle comprises a 5 storey tower house, with a longer three storey hall house, providing a substantial range of accommodation. At basement level are the remains of cellars and a kitchen with a large fireplace and water inlet. Above this is the large hall. This is connected to a large drawing room in the tower house, which retains its stone floor and large fireplace with carved stone decoration. A broad stair rises from the entrance to the hall, contained in a small tower to the north-west. A second smaller stair leads up from the hall to the parapet walk on three sides of the tower house. Upper rooms would have contained bedrooms

The exterior displays numerous "double keyhole" gunloops, as well as decorative string courses and corbelling. Over the entrance are blank panels framed by carved supports, as well as the arms of the 5th Earl of Argyll with the motto DIA LE UA NDUIBHNE, "God be with O'Duine", referring to the semi-legendary ancestors of Clan Campbell. At the top of the tower are the remains of open rounds along the parapet, and a caphouse above the stair. Fragments of carved drain spouts have been found, and are on display in the cellars.

To the south and west is a partially walled courtyard garden. An archway bears the inscription SDC LHL 1681, for Sir Duncan Campbell, 4th Baronet and Lady Henrietta Lindsay, whose support for Argyll's uprising led to the castle's destruction.

References

- Coventry, Martin *The Castles of Scotland (3rd Edition)*, Goblinshead, 2001
- Lindsay, Maurice *The Castles of Scotland*, Constable & Co. 1986
- Walker, Frank Arneil *The Buildings of Scotland: Argyll and Bute*, Penguin, 2000
- Historic Scotland Listed building report [1]
- National Monuments Record of Scotland Site Reference NM80SW 2 [2]

External links

- Carnasserie Castle - site information from Historic Scotland [3]
- Gazetteer for Scotland: Carnasserie Castle [4]
- RCAHMS Images on line [5]
- Panorama from Carnassarie Castle [6] (QuickTime required).

Skipness Castle

Skipness Castle

Skipness Castle	
Kintyre Peninsula, Scotland; near the village of Skipness	
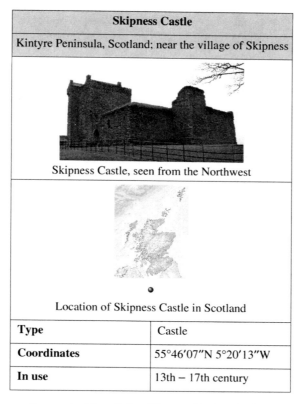 Skipness Castle, seen from the Northwest Location of Skipness Castle in Scotland	
Type	Castle
Coordinates	55°46′07″N 5°20′13″W
In use	13th – 17th century

Skipness Castle stands on the east side of the Kintyre Peninsula in Scotland near the village of Skipness.

History

The main structure of the castle was built in the early 13th century by the Clan MacSween with later fortifications and other additions made to the castle through the 13th, 14th and 16th centuries.

The castle was garrisoned with royal troops in 1494 during King James IV of Scotland's suppression of the Isles. Archibald Campbell, 2nd Earl of Argyll granted Skipness to his younger son Archibald Campbell in 1511.

During the Wars of the Three Kingdoms in 1646, the castle was sieged by forces under the command of Alasdair Mac Colla. During the siege, Alasdair's brother, Gilleasbuig Mac Colla, was killed in August 1646.

The castle was abandoned in the 17th century.

External links

- Skipness Castle - site information from Historic Scotland [1]

Geographical coordinates: 55°46′07″N 5°20′13″W

Claig Castle

Claig Castle

Claig Castle was a stronghold of the Clan Donald or **MacDonald** in the south of Scotland.

History

The castle was once a massive fort described as a *sea fortress*, which allowed the Macdonald Lord of the Isles to dominate and control the sea traffic north and south through the Hebrides for more than four centuries.

The castle remained a stronghold of the MacDonalds until they were subdued in the 17th century by the Clan Campbell.

Location

The castle is located at grid reference NR471627 on the Isle of Fraoch Eilean which is just off the Isle of Jura, Scotland.

See also

- Castles in Scotland A list of Scottish castles.
- Clan Donald

External links

- http://www.theisleofjura.co.uk/index%20files/Clans/MacDonald.html [1]
- http://www.theisleofjura.co.uk/web_365/Claig%20Castle.html [2]

Geographical coordinates: 55°47′29″N 6°2′7″W

Dunaverty Castle

Dunaverty Castle

Dunaverty Castle is a castle at Southend, Kintyre in Scotland and was once a fort belonging to the Clan Donald or **MacDonald**.

History

The remains of Dunaverty Castle stand on a rocky head land on the south east corner of Kintyre, Scotland. The headland it was built on forms a natural stronghold with the sea on three sides and is only approachable from the north. It is attached to the mainland only by a narrow path. It is known that the castle itself was accessed by a drawbridge.

13th Century

In 1248 King Henry of England allowed Walter Bissett to buy stores from Ireland for Dunaverty Castle which he had seized and was fortifying, apparently in revenge for hospitality given by King Alexander II of Scotland to certain English pirates. However during that same year the castle was taken by Allan, the son of the Earl of Atholl and Bissett was taken prisoner.

In 1263 Dunaverty Castle was garrisoned by King Alexander III of Scotland during the Norse invasion by King Haakon IV of Norway. The castle was eventually surrendered to the Norwegian King. Eventually the Norwegian King gave the castle to Dugall MacRuairi the founder of Clan MacDougall. Dugall or Dougall was the grandson of Ranald who was in turn the son of the rival Scottish King Somerled the ancestor of all MacDonalds and MacDougalls. The castle is believed to have soon become property of Alexander MacDonald of Isla.

14th century

It is believed that King Robert I of Scotland also known as Robert the Bruce escaped his enemies by sailing down the Firth of Clyde until he reached safety at Dunaverty Castle. There he spent several days hospitably entertained by Angus Og of Islay. The King of Scotland however soon needed to flee to Rathlin Island off the coast of Ireland in order to escape the pursuing English fleet. On the 22nd of September 1306 the English King ordered the employment of miners, crossbowmen and masons in the siege of Dunaverty Castle which was soon surrendered.

15th Century

In 1493 the fourth and last Lord of the Isles forfeited his title to King James IV of Scotland. By 1494 the King had garrisoned and provisioned Dunaverty Castle. It is said that the MacDonalds led by Sir John MacDonald, who the king had recently knighted, retook the castle before the King had even departed to Stirling and that the dead body of the King's castle governor was hung over the castle walls in sight of the King and his departing entourage. Sir John Macdonald however was later captured by MacIain of Ardnamurchan. He was tried and hung on the Burgh Muir.

16th Century

The castle was repaired by the crown between 1539 and 1542. In January 1544, a Commission in Queen Mary's name was given to the Captain, Constable and Keeper of the Castle of Dunaverty, to deliver it with its artillery and ammunition to the Earl of Argyll and in April of that year Argyll received a 12-year tack of North and South Kintyre, including the Castle. The castle was attacked by the Earl of Surrey in 1588 but no damage was done.

17th Century

In 1626, the Lordship of Kintyre was reconstituted in favour of the Earl of Argyll and Dunaverty Castle was denoted as its principal message. Argyll bestowed the Lordship of Kintyre on James, his eldest son by his second marriage, who, in 1635, at Dunaverty, granted a charter of the Lordship to Viscount Dunluce, eldest son of the first Earl of Antrim but the transfer was set aside by the Scottish Privy Council, no doubt on a complaint by Argyll's eldest son, the Marquis of Lorn, who had bitterly resented his father's bestowal of the Lordship on his younger half-brother. On 12 December 1636, Lom received a charter, under the Great Seal, of the Lordship of Kintyre, with the Castle of Dunaverty as its principal message

During the Civil War it was besieged in 1647 by Scottish supporters of Oliver Cromwell who were led by General David Leslie from Clan Leslie (Leslie later became a Royalist). The MacDonalds surrendered and then 300 of them were massacred. The castle is nothing more than a ruin now, known as **Blood Rock**. This incident became known as the Dunaverty Massacre.

See also

- Castles in Scotland
- Clan Donald

External links

- http://www.highlandconnection.org/castles/dunavertycastle.html [1]
- http://www.visitkintyre.info/places/Southend/ [2]

Geographical coordinates: 55°18′27″N 5°38′41″W

Castle Toward

Castle Toward

Castle Toward is an outdoor education facility, based in a nineteenth century country house on the southern tip of the Cowal peninsula in Argyll, Scotland.

Castle Toward

History

Ruins of Toward Castle

Toward Castle

The original Toward Castle dates from the 15th century. Now ruined, it was owned by the Clan Lamont until 1809. The ruins lie around 500 metres (1600 ft) south-east of the later building.

Castle Toward

The present Castle Toward was built in 1820 by Kirkman Finlay, former Lord Provost of Glasgow, as his family's country house. Later owned and extended by the Coats family of Paisley, the house is a castellated mansion, with Italian plasterwork installed in the public rooms in 1920. The grounds incorporate the ruins of the sixteenth century Toward Castle, the Chinese ponds, wooded areas, access to the shore, and views over the Firth of Clyde.

During the Second World War the castle was used as a combined operations centre (COC No. 2), HMS *Brontosaurus*.

With the reorganisation of local government in Scotland in 1996, ownership passed to Argyll and Bute Council and such centres were threatened with closure. A rescue operation was mounted by Castle Toward's then principal, Peter Wilson, and a company, Actual Reality was formed, which kept the castle in use as an outdoor activity centre, along with the council-owned centre at Ardentinny. There have been several attempts by the council to sell the estate, but all have met with fierce opposition.

On 13th November 2009 Argyll and Bute Council closed the castle on the grounds that it was unfit for purpose. This followed directly Actual Reality's request to upgrade the fire protection system following an audit of the castle in co-operation with Strathclyde Fire Brigade. There is currently a growing online campaign to save Castle Toward, including a Facebook campaign which has attracted over 4000 members in its first month.

Current uses

Toward Castle is now a residential training centre operated by Actual Reality. Outdoor education activities include high ropes, kayaking, and orienteering, as well as gorge walks and hill walks. For younger children there are wide games, amongst other outdoor games. Its long history has led to a multitude of ghost stories, much perpetuated by the young people who visit.

The grounds of the outdoor education centre were used as a location for the children's BBC Television series *Raven*, featuring the actor James MacKenzie, up to and including the seventh series at the start of 2008.

Footnotes

Geographical coordinates: 55°52′10″N 5°0′53″W

Torosay Castle

Torosay Castle

Torosay Castle is a large house situated 1½ miles south of Craignure on the Isle of Mull, in the Scottish Inner Hebrides.

It was designed by architect David Bryce for John Campbell of Possil (see Carter-Campbell of Possil) in the Scottish Baronial style, and completed in 1858. Torosay is surrounded by 12 acres (49000 m^2) of spectacular gardens including formal terraces laid out at the turn of the 20th century and attributed to Sir Robert Lorimer. While remaining a family home, the castle and gardens are open to the public, being linked to the Craignure ferry terminal by the Isle of Mull Railway.

The garden's Statue Walk is made up of 19 statues in the style of Italian sculptor Antonio Bonazza. The statues were acquired by then-owner Walter Murray Guthrie from a derelict garden near Milan and shipped to Scotland for next to nothing as ballast in a cargo ship.

Torosay Castle

John Campbell of Possil sold the castle and the estate to Arburthnot Charles Guthrie, a wealthy London businessman, in 1865. It served as his "getaway" and must have been ideal for that purpose, as the castle has over 60 rooms and is surrounded by an estate of over 12 acres (0.049 km^2). The current owner is now the sixth generation of the Guthrie family to live in the castle. Following the sale of Guthrie Castle out of the Guthrie family, Torosay is now generally acknowledged as the seat for Clan Guthrie.

Champagne find

In July 2008 the then oldest bottle of Veuve Clicquot champagne was discovered inside a sideboard in Torosay Castle. The 1893 bottle was in mint condition, having been kept in the dark sideboard since at least 1897. The champagne is now on display at the Veuve Clicquot visitor centre in Reims, France, and regarded as "priceless".

External links

- Torosay Castle [1]

Geographical coordinates: 56°27′18″N 5°41′14″W

Coeffin

Coeffin

Castle Coeffin is a ruin on the island of Lismore, an island in Loch Linnhe, in Argyll, on the west coast of Scotland. It stands on a promontory on the north-west coast of the island, across Loch Linnhe from Glensanda, at grid reference NM853437.

Castle Coeffin ruins

History

Coeffin Castle was built in the 13th century, probably by the MacDougalls of Lorn. Lismore was an important site within their lordship, being the location of St. Moluag's Cathedral, seat of the Bishop of Argyll. The first written evidence of the castle occurs in 1469–70, when it was granted to Sir Colin Campbell of Glenorchy by Colin Campbell, 1st Earl of Argyll. It is unlikely to have been occupied in post-mediaeval times.

The ruins

The ruins comprise an oblong hall-house and an irregularly shaped bailey. The hall is an irregular rectangle, measuring 20.3 by 10.4 metres (67 by 34 ft) The walls are from 2.1 to 2.4 metres (6 ft 10 in to 7 ft 10 in) thick. The bailey was mostly built at a later date than the hall. An external stair probably linked the entrance, in the north-east wall, to the bailey. A second door gave access to the sea to the south-west.

Other features

A tidal fish trap, of unknown age, is located in the small bay to the south-east of the castle. To the north-east of the castle are the remains of a stone-walled fort. The *Ordnance Gazetteer of Scotland*, published in 1892, lists a Castle Rachal in the same general location as Castle Coeffin. It is described as "a very ancient Scandinavian fortalice in Lismore and Appin parish, Argyllshire, on the NW side of Lismore island, 2.5 miles from the north-eastern extremity, now a dilapidated ivy-clad ruin."

References

Geographical coordinates: 56°32′10″N 5°29′36″W

Castle Sween

Castle Sween

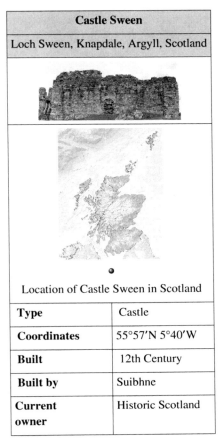

Castle Sween	
Loch Sween, Knapdale, Argyll, Scotland	
Location of Castle Sween in Scotland	
Type	Castle
Coordinates	55°57′N 5°40′W
Built	12th Century
Built by	Suibhne
Current owner	Historic Scotland

Castle Sween is located on the eastern shore of Loch Sween, in Knapdale, on the west coast of Argyll, Scotland. Castle Sween is thought to be one of the earliest stone castles built in Scotland, having been built sometime in the late twelfth century. The castle's towers were later additions to wooden structures which have now since vanished.

History

Castle Sween takes its name from Suibhne, (Anglicized as *Sween*), who is thought to have built the castle. Suibhne was thought to have been a grandson of Hugh the Splendid O'Neill who died in 1047.

In the thirteenth century the Clan MacSween, or descendants Suibhne, governed lands extending as far north as Loch Awe and as far south as Skipness Castle on Loch Fyne. In the later half of the thirteenth century the MacSween lands of Knapdale passed into the hands of the Stewart Earls of Menteith.

By the time of the Wars of Scottish Independence the MacSweens took the wrong side, and when Robert the Bruce became King of Scotland he displaced the MacSweens from their lands. After Robert the Bruce had defeated MacDougall Lord of Lorne in 1308, he then laid siege to Alasdair Og MacDonald in Castle Sween. Alastair gave himself up and was disinherited by Robert Bruce who then granted Islay to Alasdair's younger brother, Angus Og, the king's loyal supporter, who also received the Castle Sween in Kintyre from the King.

In 1310, Edward II of England granted John MacSween and his brothers their family's ancestral lands of Knapdale, (though by then Castle Sween was held by Sir John Menteith). It is possible that this could be the "*tryst of a fleet against Castle Sween*", recorded in the Book of the Dean of Lismore, which tells of the attack of John Mac Sween on Castle Sween.

In 1323, after the death of Sir John Menteith, the Lordship of Arran and Knapdale passed to his son and grandson. In 1376 half of Knapdale, which included Castle Sween, passed into possession of the MacDonald Lords of the Isles, by grant of Robert II of Scotland to his son-in-law John I, Lord of the Isles.

During the MacDonald's century and a half of holding the castle, the castellans were first MacNeils and later MacMillans.

In 1490 Castle Sween was granted to Colin Campbell, 1st Earl of Argyll, by James IV of Scotland.

In the 1640s, during the Wars of the Three Kingdoms, Castle Sween was attacked and burnt by Alasdair MacColla and his Irish Confederate followers.

In 1933 the castle was put in the care of the Historic Building and Monuments Directorate (HBMD). Currently Castle Sween is under the protection of Historic Scotland.

External links

* Castle Sween - site information from Historic Scotland [1]

55°56′52″N 5°39′51″W

Achallader Castle

Achallader Castle

Achallader Castle is a ruined 16th century tower house under the shadow of Beinn Achaladair, about 3.5 miles north of Bridge of Orchy, Argyll, Scotland. Its name is from Gaelic, meaning field of hard water.

History

The tower originally belonged to the Fletcher family, but Sir Duncan Campbell of Glen Orchy, built most of the existing tower, which he acquired in 1590. The MacGregors burnt the castle in 1603.

In the summer of 1683 a Commission for the settlement of the Highlands, led by Sir William Drummond of Cromlix stayed at the castle, welcoming, among others McIain, the future victim, with his clan, of the massacre of Glencoe.

In 1689, with William and Mary now reigning, the McIain's returning from their victory at Killiecrankie and repulse at Dunkeld, pulled down what they could of the castle. It was never restored.

In June 1691 John, Earl of Breadalbane, empowered by King William to treat with the clans, conferred with the highland chiefs in the ruin of the castle. By a mixture of threats, promises of bribes, and duplicity, he persuaded most of the clans -but not the McIains - to enter a treaty. This included secret provisions, which he later denied, including the right of the chiefs to request relief from their oaths of allegiance from the exiled James VII and II. The promised bribes did not materialise.

Description

The castle formerly rose to three storeys and a garret, well defended by shot-holes. Now only two walls, one with a trace of corbelling, remain, sheltering the farm buildings of Achallader Farm.

Tradition

It is said that when the Fletchers owned Achallader, Sir Duncan Campbell - known as Black Duncan - ordered an English servant (or soldier) to pasture his horse in the Fletchers' corn. When warned off by the Fletchers - in Gaelic - he did not understand; when he did not remove his horse they shot him. Black Duncan, affecting concern that the Fletcher laird would be hanged for the killing, advised him to flee to France. Before he fled he passed the property to Black Duncan, supposedly until his return, to prevent it being forfeited to the Crown. The Fletchers never recovered the property.

Yes this may well be the tradition however the real truth is that Black Duncan knew there was a change in the law coming so he sent our chief off claimed the land and then massacred our clan at Glen Aray in the wee Hamlet of Drimfern. This perpetuation of the great Campbell name is nauseating the chief should hand the castle back because deception is a criminal offence and he has inherited land that was taken by deception.

Bibliography

- *The Castles of Scotland*, Martin Coventry, Goblinshead, 2001
- *The Munros*, Cameron McNeish, Lomond Books, 1996
- *Glencoe*, John Prebble, Penguin, 1966.

Geographical coordinates: 56°33′46″N 4°43′34″W

Rothesay Castle

Rothesay Castle

Rothesay Castle is a ruined castle in Rothesay, the principal town on the Isle of Bute, in western Scotland. Located at NS086646, the castle has been described as "one of the most remarkable in Scotland", for its long history dating back to the beginning of the 13th century, and its unusual circular plan.

The castle comprises a huge curtain wall, strengthened by four round towers, together with a 16th century forework, the whole surrounded by a broad moat. Built by the Stewart family, it survived Norse attacks to

Rothesay Castle, with the 16th century forework in the centre, and the 13th century "Pigeon Tower" on the right.

become a royal residence. Though falling into ruin after the 17th century, the castle was repaired by the Marquess of Bute before passing into state care last century.

The early castle

The castle was built either by Alan, High Steward of Scotland (d.1204), or by his son Walter Stewart (d.1246), ancestor of the House of Stuart or Stewart. Alan was granted the lands of the Isle of Bute by William I in 1200. A wooden castle was constructed first, but the stone circular curtain wall was in place by the 1230s, when the castle was attacked and taken by Norsemen under Gillespec MacDougall (known as Uspak in Norse), grandson of Somerled. According to *The Saga of Haakon Haakonsson*, the Norsemen fought for three days to take the castle, breaking down part of the eastern wall by hewing the stone with their axes, and certainly the eastern wall shows signs of damage. This saga is the earliest recorded account of an assault on a Scottish castle. In 1263, Rothesay was taken again by the Norse under Haakon IV before the Battle of Largs. Although the Battle of Largs was indecisive, Haakon's campaign was unsuccessful, and effectively ended Norse influence in western Scotland.

The early castle comprised only the roughly circular curtain wall, 3m thick and around 43m across, built on a low mound, with a battlement on top accessed by open stairs. The moat was connected to the sea, the shoreline being some 100m further north-east than today. The broad crenellations can be made out within the walls, which were

The 13th century curtain wall seen from the south-east, across the moat. The bases of the south-east and south-west towers can be seen.

later raised. Holes in the upper wall would have supported a timber bretasche, a projecting structure serving as an extended battlement. This curtain wall was built of coursed ashlar, and had only two openings in its length. The main gate was an arched opening with a simple timber door. The second opening was a small postern gate in the west wall, later blocked.

In the later part of the 13th century, the castle was strengthened by the addition of four round towers, of which only the north-east survives intact. These three-storey towers had strong splayed bases, with arrow slits below the crenellated parapet. A portcullis was added to the main gate.

Wars of independence and the rise of the Stewarts

During the Wars of Scottish Independence, Rothesay was held by the English, but was taken by Robert the Bruce in 1311. It then returned to English hands in 1334, before being taken again by the Scots. Following the accession of the Stewarts to the throne of Scotland in 1371, the castle became a favourite residence of kings Robert II and Robert III, who died here in 1406. Robert II granted the hereditary keepership of the castle to his son John, ancestor of the Earls and Marquesses of Bute. Robert III made his eldest son David Duke of Rothesay in 1401, beginning a tradition of honouring the heir to the throne of Scotland with this title. In 1462 the castle survived a siege by the forces of John of Islay, Earl of Ross and the last Lord of the Isles.

16th and 17th centuries

In the early 16th century Rothesay Castle was strengthened again. Construction of a gatehouse keep, extending from the north of the curtain wall, began around the turn of the century, to provide more modern accommodation for James IV. The curtain wall itself was raised up to ten metres in height, the works continuing into the reign of James V. In 1527 the castle withstood another siege by the Master of Ruthven, which destroyed much of the burgh of Rothesay. In 1544, the castle fell to the Earl of Lennox, acting for the English during the so-called "Rough Wooing".

The forework is an L-plan structure, which jutted into the moat and was accessed by a drawbridge. The lower floor comprised a vaulted entrance tunnel running into the older castle courtyard. Above, the four storey tower contained royal lodgings, and still bears the royal coat of arms above the door. Also in the early 16th century, a chapel was constructed inside the old castle. Simple in form, the chapel measured around 6m by 9m, and is now the only surviving structure within the curtain wall. The north-west tower was converted into a doocot, and is known as the "Pigeon Tower", due to the nest boxes built into the outside wall.

Rothesay was garrisoned for the Royalists during the Wars of the Three Kingdoms, then for the occupying forces of Oliver Cromwell, who invaded Scotland with his New Model Army in the early 1650s. On their departure in 1660, the troops partially dismantled the structure. What was left was burned by the supporters of Archibald Campbell, 9th Earl of Argyll during his rising of 1685, in support of the Monmouth Rebellion against James VII.

Repair and restoration

Following a long period of neglect, the 2nd Marquess of Bute employed 70 men to excavate the ruins, clearing large amounts of rubbish from the castle in 1816-17. But it was not until the 1870s that the ruins were stabilised. The 3rd Marquess, a keen restorer of historic buildings, embarked upon a series of repairs and restorations, following surveys and advice from his regular architect William Burges. His "restorations" continued until 1900, and include the clearing and shaping of the moat, as well as the red sandstone additions to the forework, which reinstated the hall roof while significantly altering the character of the building.

In 1961 Rothesay Castle was gifted to the state, and is now a Scheduled Ancient Monument, in the care of Historic Scotland.

The castle is open to visitors year round (current price £4.00 for adults). Fine views can be seen from the top of the walls over the town and back towards the mainland.

References

- Coventry, Martin *The Castles of Scotland (3rd Edition)*, Goblinshead, 2001
- Lindsay, Maurice *The Castles of Scotland*, Constable & Co. 1986
- Tabraham, Chris *Scotland's Castles*, BT Batsford/Historic Scotland, 1997
- Walker, Frank Arneil *The Buildings of Scotland: Argyll and Bute*, Penguin, 2000
- Historic Scotland Listed Building Report [1]
- National Monuments Record of Scotland Site Reference NS06SE 3 [2]

External links

- Rothesay Castle - site information from Historic Scotland [3]

Geographical coordinates: 55°50′12″N 5°03′29″W

Dunderave Castle

Dunderave Castle

Dunderave Castle is an L-plan castle built in the 16th century as the Scottish seat of the MacNaughton clan. The castle lies on a small promontory on the northern shores of Loch Fyne, around 5 kilometres (3.1 mi) north-east of Inveraray, Argyll. The castle is in use as a residence. The present castle was built after their previous castle was destroyed following a Plague infection. The old castle, and remnants of McNaughton crannógs, can still be seen on the lochan known as the Dubh Loch at the head of Glen Shira.

Dunderave Castle

The name Dunderave is of Gaelic origin. Since the MacNachtans were designated 'of Dunderave' from as early as 1473, the place-name appears to have moved with the clan from the Dubh Loch. It has been suggested that the name derives either from Dun-an-Rudha, meaning 'The Knoll on the Promontory', or else from Dun-da-Ramh, 'The Castle of Two Oars'. The latter is taken to imply that there was a ferry near the site of the castle.

See also

- Fraoch Eilean, Loch Awe - earlier MacNauchtan castle
- Dundarave House - the Irish seat of the MacNaughton clan

Bibliography

- Cock, Matthew (1998), *Dunderave Castle and the MacNachtans of Argyll*, Dunderave Estate, ISBN 0965833801

External links

- Overview of Dundarave Castle [1] from the Gazetteer for Scotland
- Dundarave Castle in the 1900s [2]

Geographical coordinates: 56°14′35″N 4°59′53″W

Kilmahew Castle

Kilmahew Castle

Kilmahew Castle	
Cardross, Argyll and Bute, Scotland NS350786	
Kilmahew Castle	
Type	Rectangular tower house
Built	unknown, but after 1290
Built by	unknown member of the Clan Napier
Construction materials	Stone
In use	15th century to 21st century
Current condition	Ruin
Current owner	Catholic Church
Open to the public	Yes
Controlled by	Clan Napier until 1820 various owners 1820 to present

Kilmahew Castle is a ruined castle located just north of Cardross, in the council area of Argyll and Bute. Kilmahew is named for its patron saint, Mochta (Mahew).

History

Kilmahew castle was built upon the lands granted to the Napiers by Malcolm, the Earl of Lennox around the year 1290. The castle itself was built sometime in the 16th century by the Napier family, who owned it for the next 18 generations. The Napiers who owned Kilmahew are notable for being the progenitors of most of the Napiers in North America, as well as some of their members who had notable contributions in the field of engineering, such as Robert Napier, the "Father of Clyde Shipbuilding," and David, James and Montague Napier, who owned the engineering company of Napier & Son.

The estate was inherited by George Maxwell of Newark and Tealing (1678-1744) in 1694, when he assumed the name of his maternal grandfather, John Napier of Kilmahew. The estate was sold to Alexander Sharp in 1820 in repayment of gambling debts. In 1839, the estate was acquired by James Burns.

The ruins were acquired by the Archdiocese of Glasgow, along with the surrounding estate, in 1948.

Design

The castle was originally a four-storey 16th century tower house. Some obvious gothic modifications were done during the 19th century by Alexander Sharp, who owned the castle at the time.

External links

- a site with some pictures of the ruin [1]
- Annals of Garelochside, which contains some descriptions of the ruin [2]

Geographical coordinates: 55°58′19″N 4°38′44″W

Kames Castle

Kames Castle

Kames Castle is a castellated mansion house on the Isle of Bute, Scotland.

On the shore of Kames Bay near Port Bannatyne, the castle consists of a 14th Century tower, with a house built on it in the 18th Century. The Castle is set in 20 acres (81000 m^2) of planted grounds, including a two-acre 18th Century walled garden.

Kames Castle

Originally the seat of the Bannatyne family, Kames is one of the oldest continuously inhabited houses in Scotland.

Owners

Sir William Macleod Bannatyne (Lord Bannatyne) (1743-1833) was a distinguished lawyer and judge in Edinburgh. He lost his fortune and was forced to sell Kames in 1812.

James Hamilton bought Kames Castle in 1812.

Kames was the birthplace, and early home of the critic and essayist John Sterling. Thomas Carlyle in his biography refers to the castle as 'a kind of dilapidated baronial residence to which a small farm was then attached'.

Today the castle is privately occupied with a number of cottages available as holiday lets.

Footnotes

Geographical coordinates: 55°51′44″N 5°5′45″W

Tullichewan

Tullichewan

Tullichewan is a former estate in the Vale of the river Leven, near Loch Lomond, Scotland.

History

Originally called Tuloch Eoghain, "the hill of Eoghan." In the 17th century it was acquired by the Colquhoun family, and was known as Tully-Colquhoun or Tillyquhoun; and then Tullichewan. The Tullichewan estate was sold by the Colquhoun clan to James Buchanan in 1792.

Tullichewan Castle was designed in 1792 by architect Robert Lugar, who also designed Balloch Castle. It is the first example in Scotland of an asymmetrical Gothic house. The Horrocks family purchased the castle in 1817, living there until 1843. The estate was then sold to William Campbell of J & W Campbell, Glasgow merchants and remained in the Campbell family until the twentieth century.

The last owner was J Scott Anderson who acquired the house around 1930. At the outbreak of World War II, Tullichewan Castle Estate was requisitioned by the Royal Navy, who retained it for the rest of the war. Tullichewan Castle Camp was put to various uses. After the war, it was used as accommodation for workers at the Royal Naval Torpedo Factory in Alexandria. Mr J Scott Anderson returned to live in the castle, until its upkeep became too much. The castle then lay abandoned until it was finally demolished demolished by explosives in 1954.

Although modern development has consumed most of the former estate, and little remains, a number of remnants are reported to have survived. The A82 dual carriageway and the A811 road were built through the grounds, with housing developments and the Vale of Leven Hospital covering the estate. The former stables and a fragment of the original tower can still be seen from the A82. The north lodge, or gatehouse, has been lost in the area of Tullichewan Caravan Park, where the estate also had a walled orchard. The south lodge can still be found on Main Street, Alexandria, north of the entrance to Christie Park. Of the Camp, no trace remains.

Footnotes

Geographical coordinates: 55°59′48″N 4°36′6″W

Dunyvaig Castle

Dunyvaig Castle

Dunyvaig Castle, (Scottish Gaelic: *Dun Naomhaig*, Anglicised *Fort of the galleys*, also known as *Dunnyveg* is located on the south side of Islay, upon the shore of Lagavulin Bay, 4km from Port Ellen.

The castle was once a naval base of the Lord of the Isles, chiefs of Clan Donald. It was held by the chiefs of the Clan MacDonald of Dunnyveg. The castle was forfeited in 1493 and then passed to the MacIans of Ardnamurchan. Afterwards the castle was leased to the MacDonalds, then the Campbells and back to the MacDonalds. In the seventeenth century the castle was seized by the Covenanters and passed into the hands of the Campbells of Cawdor, who held it until 1677, when Sir Hugh Campbell destroyed the castle and moved to Islay House.

Today all that remains of the castle are mainly the ruins of the sixteenth century castle, although the site includes a thirteenth century courtyard, and a fifteenth century keep.

External links

* http://www.highlandconnection.org/castles/dunnyvegcastle.html [1]

Geographical coordinates: 55°38′01″N 6°07′23″W

Ardencaple Castle

Ardencaple Castle

Ardencaple Castle	
Rhu, Helensburgh, Argyll and Bute, Scotland	

Ardencaple Castle, 1901.

Built	original: c.12th century. rebuilt c.18th & 19th centuries.
Built by	original: unknown. rebuilt: Campbells of Argyll.
Height	remaining tower: 45 feet (13.7 m).
In use	c.12th century to 20th century. Nav aid: 1957-present.
Demolished	1957.
Current condition	1 remaining tower.
Open to the public	Grounds only.

Controlled by	*unknown* lairds of Ardincaple: c.1100s-1460s.
	MacAulay lairds of Ardincaple: c.1460s-1760s.
	Campbells of Argyll: c.1760s-1852.
	Colquhouns of Luss: 1852-1923.
	H. Stromberg-Macaulay: 1923-1931.
	Adelaide Parker Voorheis: 1931-1934.
	consortium of developers: 1934-1937.
	Royal Navy (HMNB Clyde): 1937-.

Ardencaple Castle, also known as **Ardincaple Castle**, and sometimes referred to as **Ardencaple Castle Light**, is a listed building, situated about a statute mile from Helensburgh, Argyll and Bute, Scotland. Today, all that remains of the castle is a tower, perched on the edge of a plateau, looking down on a flat tract of land between it and the shore of the Firth of Clyde. The original castle was thought to have been built sometime in the 12th century, and part of the remains of the original castle were said to have existed in the 19th century. Today, that sole remaining tower is used as a navigational aid for shipping on the Firth of Clyde. Because of its use as a lighthouse the tower has been called Ardencaple Castle Light.

Lairds of Ardincaple

The word *Ardencaple* or *Ardincaple* has been said to be derived from the Gaelic *Ard na gCapull*, meaning "cape of the horses", or "of the mares", or "height of the horses". In 1351 this place name was recorded as *Airdendgappil*. From the Middle Ages the lands of Ardencaple were controlled by the Lairds of Ardincaple. By the late 15th century or 16th century the lairds had adopted the surname *MacAulay*. By this time the Laird of Ardincaple was considered the clan chief of Clan MacAulay.

The fortunes of the Lairds of Ardincaple failed in the 18th century. These chiefs of Clan MacAulay were forced to divide and sell, piece by piece, the lands once governed by former lairds of Ardincaple. In the 1740s, Archibald MacAulay, Laird of Ardencaple, had to sell off a portion of his estate, though by the early 1750s the roof had fallen in and the overall condition of the castle had deteriorated to such an extent that the next Laird was forced to abandon his residence there and live in nearby Laggarie. In about 1767, the 12th chief, Aulay Macaulay, died at High Laggarie (now within the present village of Rhu).

Renovations to the Ardincaple Estate

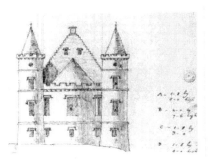

Sketch by Robert Adam of his planned
addition to Ardincaple Castle in 1774.

The estate was then purchased by John Campbell, 4th Duke of Argyll, and remained in possession of the Campbells well into the 19th century. It was during the Campbell's tenure as lairds of Ardencaple in the 18th century that extensive development was done on the estate by Robert Adam - Scotland's foremost architect of the time. In 1764, while the house was in possession of Lord Frederick Campbell, Robert Adam was first consulted about work on the castle. The house was then irregularly shaped, and Adam came up with a plan for the addition of castle-style additions on the western side of the house which faced the Gare Loch. However, nothing came of this scheme and it wasn't until 1774 that Adam came up with a set of drawings for an addition to the southern half of the west front of the house. This addition was made up of three-bay-windowed, D-shaped tower set in between two smaller turrets (*pictured left*). Later photographs of Ardincaple Castle show that Adam's extension had been altered or that some features present in his sketch were omitted from being implemented. For instance, the conical roofs, the crow-stepped gable in the sketch do not appear in photographs of the castle. Photographs of Ardincaple Castle show that the tower and southern turret had one more storey than appear in Adam's sketch. According to David King, it is possible that Adam was responsible for the added extra floor to the tower, but that is it very unlikely Adam altered the turret because the altered turret broke the symmetry of the addition. Also, Adam had planned that the tower would contain a D-shaped dressing room on its main floor (upper floor). However, it was later decided to make the room oval shaped. David King remarks that Adam had planned a pleasant ceiling for this room, but that there is no sign of it in photographs of 1957. George Campbell, 8th Duke of Argyll was born at Ardencaple Castle on April 30, 1823. By 1852 the Duchess Dowager of Argyll sold the Ardencaple estate to the wealthy Colquhouns of Luss.

Modern era and destruction of the castle

In 1923, Sir Iain Colquhoun sold the castle to Mrs. H. Macaulay-Stromberg, a wealthy American, who restored the castle and lived there until her death, in 1931. The castle then passed to Adelaide Parker Voorheis until 1935, when it passed to a consortium of developers who had constructed, in 1936-1937 a housing estate on what used to be the Tower Lawn. The castle then was requisitioned by the Royal Navy with the outbreak of World War II.

In 1957 most of the castle was demolished by the government in order to build naval housing for the nearby HMNB Clyde (Faslane Naval Base), though one tower was left to be used as a mount for navigational beacons and transit lights for the Royal Navy. From then on, the 45-foot (13.7 m) high tower was known as "Ardencaple Castle Range Rear Light", and had two green lights mounted on its south-west corner.

Ardencaple Castle Light. Today the tower is used as a navigational aid for shipping on the Firth of Clyde.

Ardencaple Castle has been considered a Category B listed building since May 14, 1971. Today, all that remains of the grand turreted mansion is one solitary tower.

See also

- Clan MacAulay
- Rhu
- Helensburgh

References

Ardencaple Castle

Location in Scotland.

Geographical coordinates: 56°0′32.88″N 4°45′25.09″W

Achanduin Castle

Achanduin Castle

Achanduin Castle	
Achnacroish, Lismore, Argyll and Bute, Scotland.	
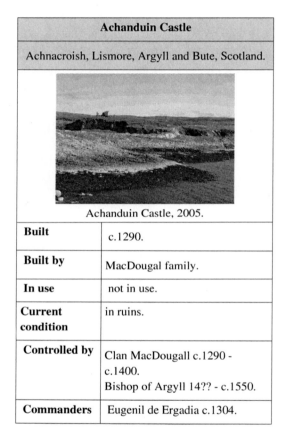 Achanduin Castle, 2005.	
Built	c.1290.
Built by	MacDougal family.
In use	not in use.
Current condition	in ruins.
Controlled by	Clan MacDougall c.1290 - c.1400. Bishop of Argyll 14?? - c.1550.
Commanders	Eugenil de Ergadia c.1304.

Achanduin Castle, (also known as **Achadun Castle** and **Acha-Dun**), is a castle, now in ruins, located about 5 kilometres west of Achnacroish on the north-western coastline of the Isle of Lismore, in Argyll and Bute, Scotland. The castle overlooks Loch Linnhe and Bernera Island. The ruins are thought to date back to the thirteenth century. Achanduin Castle had long been thought to have been built by the Bishop of Argyll, though recent research has proved this to be unlikely. The castle was likely built by the MacDougalls around 1290 who held it throughout the fourteenth century. The castle was also thought to have been held by the Bishops of Argyll until the mid sixteenth century.

Description of the ruins

The remains of the castle are seated on the summit of a limestone ridge on the north-western shore of Lismore. The south-west and south-east walls are collapsed though the north-east and a large part of the north-west wall still stand, to a maximum height of 6.7 metres. These curtain walls vary in thickness from 1.4 to 2.4 metres and enclose an area of about 22 metres square. The enclosed area would have contained at least two ranges of buildings on either side of a small courtyard, the south-east range being the mose substantial. During excavations of the site in 1970 and 1971, two doorways were found leading from the courtyard into the north-west range.

History

Throughout the thirteenth century the Diocese of Argyll and the see of Lismore were in virtual poverty. It had once been thought that the Bishop of Argyll was the builder of Achanduin Castle, though recent research shows that neither the see or the Bishop at any tme were wealthy enough to construct a castle. Recent research has points to the MacDougalls.

Archaeological excavations show that Achanduin Castle was built about 1290, at a time when the Bishop of Argyll, Laurence de Ergadia, was himself possibly a MacDougall. The first documentary evidence of the castle appears in a grant of lands dated 1304 at *Achichendone*, when *Eugenil de Ergadia*, Lord of Lorn, of *Menderaloch* and of *Lesmor* granted to Andrew, Bishop of Argyll lands next to the castle. This grant shows that Achanduin Castle was in the hands of a MacDougall at that time.

The MacDougalls were forfeit in 1308, and losing most of their lands following the Battle of the Pass of Brander and the loss of their stronghold of Dunstaffnage Castle. Of records concerning their redistributed possessions, Lismore is never mentioned. Therefore it is possible that the MacDougalls were then allowed to retain the island.

Archaeological evidence suggests that there was little occupation at the castle from c.1400 to relatively modern times.

In 1451 John Maol (*John Alani de Lorn nominato Mak Dowil*) was granted Dunolly and other lands from John Stewart, Lord of Lorn. Around this time it is believed the MacDougalls left Lismore for the mainland to build Dunollie Castle. By 1452 The Bishop of Argyll seems to have had possession of Achanduin Castle and for a short time occupied it. It is suggested that the castle may have been given to the Bishopric at an earlier time, though there was not much use for it. The evidence shows at least that the Bishop of Argyll did not frequently visit Lismore.

See also

- Clan MacDougall
- Bishop of Argyll
- Lismore

Geographical coordinates: 56°29′40″N 5°34′8″W

Finlaggan

Finlaggan

Looking southwest down Loch Finlaggan Eilean Mòr with Eilean na Comhairle more distant. Image author: Mick Garratt

Finlaggan (NR388680, Scottish Gaelic: **Port an Eilein**) is a historic site on the Eilean Mòr in Loch Finlaggan. Loch, island, and castle lie around two km to the northwest of Ballygrant on Islay.

Finlaggan was the seat of the Lords of the Isles and of Clan Donald. The site has been the subject of recent archaeological investigations and hosted an episode of Channel 4's documentary Time Team in 1995.

Two of the three islands that lie in the expansive scenery surrounding Loch Finlaggan, Eilean Mor (large island) and Eilean na Comhairle (council isle), were the ancient administration centre of the Lordship of the Isles during mostly the 13th, 14th and 15th centuries.

Still today, the islands contain remains of the buildings from where the Lords ruled the Hebrides and part of the west coast of Scotland, immensely contributing to the arts, culture and politics of Scotland.

The stone walls of a medieval chapel dedicated to St. Findlugan on Eilean Mor have been stabilised and several 16th century graves put on display and covered by large glass panels.

The Finlaggan Trust maintains the site and also refurbished a derelict cottage that has been converted into a comprehensive museum. The centre contains numerous artifacts discovered during archaeological excavations: from a sheep wool quilted aketon or under armour, to an ancient cross related to the lords. During summer 2008 the centre is being refurbished and extended.

External links

- Finlaggan Trust [1]

Geographical coordinates: 55°50′04″N 6°10′23″W

Finlaggan Castle

Finlaggan Castle

Finlaggan Castle (Scottish Gaelic: *Port an Eilein*, Anglicised: *Fort of the Island*), also known as *Eilean Mor Castle* is a ruined fortified house located on the isle of Eilean Mór on Loch Finlaggan, Islay, Scotland. It was once a residence and stronghold of Lord of the Isles and Clan Macdonald.

Built in the 13th century, with masonry walls, possibly built on the remains of an earlier Iron Age fort. The Lords of the Isles used the castle a principal court. Iain Mor MacDonald, 3rd of Dunnyveg and his son Iain Cathanach MacDonald were taken prisoner at Finlaggan Castle, through the deception of Macian of Ardnamurchan for the hanging and execution of the governor of Dunaverty Castle and were later tried and hung on the Burgh Muir, Edinburgh. In 1541 Finlaggan was held from the Crown by Donald MacGilleasbuig. The castle appears to have been demolished in the 15th-16th century.

References

- Finlaggan - The centre of the Lordship of the Isles [1]
- Site Record - Finlaggan Castle - The Royal Commission on the Ancient and Historical Monuments of Scotland [2]

Geographical coordinates: 55°50′07″N 6°10′22″W

Carrick Castle

Carrick Castle

Carrick Castle is a 15th-century tower house on the west shore of Loch Goil, Argyll, Scotland. It is located between Cuilmuich and Carrick, 4 miles (6.4 km) south of Lochgoilhead.

The Castle consists of two floors above the central great hall. The building is oblong, 66 feet long by 38 feet wide, with walls seven feet thick. It stands 64 feet high. There is a curiosity − a small chimney is built into a window recess. There is an appendage of a smaller 17th Century structure to the original rectangular tower house.

Carrick Castle

History

The present ruin is possibly the third occupant of this location. The first may have been a Viking fort. The second structure, and first castle, is believed to have been built in the 12th century. Allegedly a hunting seat of the Scots kings, Carrick was originally a Lamont stronghold. In 1368 it then passed on to the Campbell Earls of Argyll.

In the spring of 1307, Robert the Bruce drove Henry Percy from the Castle before conducting a guerrilla war against Edward I of England. Edward had given the castle, which belonged to Robert, to Percy.

The third structure, the late 15th century castle, was a royal stronghold, held by the Earls of Argyll as hereditary keepers, and was the symbol and source of their power in South Argyll. It was one of their three chief castles, the other two being Duart and Fincharn.

Mary, Queen of Scots, visited here in 1563.

In 1685, during the rebellion of Archibald Campbell, 9th Earl of Argyll, against King James VII, HMS Kingfisher bombarded the castle, badly damaging the keep, which lost its roof.

The castle was intermittently occupied until it was sold to the Murrays, the Earls of Dunmore.

The keep was a ruin for many years but is now in private ownership and undergoing restoration.

The castle

The castle stands on a rocky peninsular, and was formerly defended to landward by a ditch and drawbridge. The building is around 66 by 38 feet (20 by 12 m), and up to 64 feet (20 m) high.

References

- Carrick Castle [1], Listed Building Report
- G. Ewart and F. Baker. (1996) "Carrick Castle: symbol and source of Campbell power in south Argyll from the 14th to the 17th century [2]", *Proceedings of the Society of Antiquaries of Scotland*, Vol.128, pp.937-1016

External links

- Carrick Castle [3], Dark Isle

Geographical coordinates: 56°6′31.25″N 4°54′13.75″W

Craignish Castle

Craignish Castle

Craignish Castle, Adfern, Argyllshire, an old baronial architectural build, rebuilt around 1832. Scottish seat of the Gascoigne family of Parlington Hall, Lotherton and Castle Oliver.

Craignish Castle, standing on the peninsula, 2¼ miles from the point, includes a strong old fortalice, which withstood a six weeks' siege by Colkitto, but is mostly a good modern mansion, rebuilt about 1832; its owner, Fred. Chs. Trench-Gascoigne (b. 1814), holds 5591 acres in the shire, valued at £1013 per annum.

Craignish Castle

The founder of the Campbells of Craignish, Dugall Maul Campbell became first Laird of Craignish and his descendants built and resided in Craignish Castle in Argyll. Ranald MacCallum was made hereditary keeper of Craignish Castle in 1510. However, the castle has long since escaped family hands, and in 1832 was rebuilt as a private mansion for Mr. Trench-Gascoigne, who owned nearly 6000 acres (24 km²) in Argyllshire. Today, the Castle has been converted into apartments and is owned privately.

Lairds of Craignish

- Dugall Maul Campbell, 1st Laird (1156-????), 1st Chieftain of Campbell of Craignish
- Dougall Campbell, 2nd Laird (1178-1220), 2nd Chieftain
- Dougald Campbell, 3rd Laird (1200-1250), 3rd Chieftain
- Dougall Campbell, 4th Laird (1225-1250), 4th Chieftain
- Malcolm Campbell, 5th Laird (1250-1290), 5th Chieftain
- Dougald Campbell, 6th Laird (1272-????), 6th Chieftain
- Dougald Campbell, 7th Laird (1300-1350), 7th Chieftain

- Christina Campbell, 8th Chieftain
- Ronald Campbell, 8th Laird, 9th Chieftain
- Iain 'Gorm' Campbell, 9th Laird, 10th Chieftain
- Donald Campbell, 10th Laird, 11th Chieftain
- John Campbell, 11th Laird, 2nd Baron of Barrichibean, 12th Chieftain

- Donald Campbell, 3rd Baron, 13th Chieftain
- Iain Campbell, 4th Baron, 14th Chieftain
- Ronald Campbell, 5th Baron, 15th Chieftain
- John Campbell, 6th Baron, 16th Chieftain
- Donald Campbell, 7th Baron, 17th Chieftain
- George Campbell, 8th Baron, 18th Chieftain
- Dugald Campbell, 9th Baron, 19th Chieftain
- Captain Dugald Campbell, 10th Baron, 20th Chieftain
- Colin Campbell, 11th Baron, 21st Chieftain

The seventh laird left only one daughter, Christine Campbell (b. 1323). Her weakness and imprudence caused the majority of the estate to be resigned to the Knight of Lochow, who took advantage of her. She was left with only a small portion of the upper part of Craignish under his superiority. The nearest male representative - Ronald Campbell - fought hard to win back his heritage, and the then Chief of Clan Campbell was obliged to allow him possession of a considerable portion of the estate, but retaining the superiority, and inserting a condition in the grant that if there was ever no male heir in the direct line the lands were to revert automatically to the Argyll family. In 1544 the direct line ended, and the rightful heir, a collateral relative by the name of Charles Campbell of Corranmore in Craignish had the misfortune to kill Gillies of Glenmore in a brawl. This compelled him to flee to Perthshire where he settled at Lochtayside under the protection of the Breadalbane family. This unfortunate event therefore prevented Charles from claiming the estate, and so it fell into the hands of the Earls (later Dukes) of Argyll. Charles' descendants at Killin, Perthshire were later recognised by the Lord Lyon as Chieftains of the Clan Tearlach branch of Clan Campbell and from them descended the Campbells of Inverneill. A grandson of Duncan Campbell 8th of Inverneill in the 1980s owned one of the apartments at Craignish Castle. The arms of Campbell of Inverneill are those of Campbell of Craignish differenced by the addition of "a bordure azure" (a blue border). The first and third Campbells of Inverneill (Sir Archibald Campbell of Inverneill and Sir Janes Campbell of Inverneill Bt were interred at Westminster Abbey in what is now known as Poets Corner. The second, Sir James Campbell of Inverneill and many succeeding Campbells of Inverneill are interred in the Campbell of Inverneill Mausoleum, though the late Dr John Lorne Campbell of Inverneill (and of Canna) is interred on the Isle of Canna where he had lived for over 50 years. The estates of Inverneill, with the exception of the Mausoleum and Inverneill Island, were sold in the 1950s. Inverneill Island remains in the ownership of the present Campbell of Inverneill.

One part of the inheritance which did not revert to the Argylls was the small Barony of Barrichibean, which John Campbell had inherited from his mother's father. This Barony is not currently possessed by anyone today, but genealogical records point to some likely successors.

Edmund Kempt Campbell was created first Baron Campbell of Craignish by the Duke of Saxe-Coburg-Gotha in 1848. He moved to America but was naturalised in Britain some years later. In 1882, Captain Ronald Macleay Lorentz Campbell, his nephew, was ennobled as Baron Craignish by the Duke of Saxe-Coburg-Gotha and applied to Queen Victoria to use the title in Britain. His application was accepted and he was allowed the title 'Baron Campbell von Laurents'. One of these barons was a hero in the Battle of Gravelotte during the Franco-Prussian war. His son Ronald also used the title, and then it fell to his granddaughter Sarah Elizabeth to become a Peeress In Her Own Right. Baroness Campbell von Laurents published a book in 1913 called 'My Motor Milestones: How to Tour in a Car', and was a member of the Italian Greyhound Club. Her father visited the famous Wright brothers, the inventors of the aeroplane, and a copy of his calling card is preserved in a collection dedicated to the aviators.

- Edmund Kempt Laurentz Campbell, 1st Baron of Craignish
- Captain Ronald Macleay Lorentz Campbell, 2nd Baron (Campbell von Laurents)
- Ronald Campbell, 3rd Baron (Campbell von Laurents)
- Sarah Elizabeth Campbell, Baroness (Campbell von Laurents)

Incumbent

The title 'Laird of Craignish' is no longer used, because the title 'Laird' conveys a sense of ownership of land, and the Craignish estates were lost long ago (see above). However, most of these properties have since been sold on.

The House of Craignish represents thousands of Campbells worldwide, but currently no Chieftain has been identified.

The title 'Baron Campbell von Laurents' is a German title, which was restricted in inheritance to the male line of the original holder, meaning it is now extinct.

Sources
- "Parish of Craignish" [1]. Gazetteer for Scotland. 2002-2008. Retrieved 2009-07-26.
- Parlington Hall the home of the Gascoigne Family who bought Craignish in 1852 for £26,000 Parlington Hall [2]

Geographical coordinates: 56°9′18″N 5°35′23″W

Moy Castle

Moy Castle

Lochbuie House and Moy Castle

Clan Maclean \ Maclaine
Branches
Maclean of Duart · Maclean of Coll · Maclean of Ardgour
Lands
Ardgour · Coll ·
Castles
Duart Castle · Glensanda Castle
Septs
Beath · Beaton · Black · Garvie · Lean · MacBeath · MacBheath · MacBeth · MacEachan · Macilduy · MacLaine · McLean · MacLergain · Maclergan · MacRankin · MacVeagh · MacVey · Rankin

Moy Castle is an extant, but badly damaged castle near Lochbuie, Mull.

History

Moy Castle was built in the 15th century by Hector Reaganach Maclean, 1st Laird of Lochbuie, brother of Lachlan Lubanach Maclean of Duart. It has a three level tower with a garret. The ground floor contains a well. It was captured from the Macleans of Lochbuie by Clan Campbell, but later returned to the Maclaines. It was abandoned in 1752 when a new house was built.

It was used for scenes in Powell and Pressburger's 1945 film *I Know Where I'm Going!*, and a group of 40 fans visited to celebrate the 60th anniversary of the film's release in 2005..

See also

- Moy Hall - an unrelated mansion near Inverness

References

Geographical coordinates: 56°21′21″N 5°51′31″W

Tarbert Castle

Tarbert Castle

Tarbert Castle is located on the southern shore of Tarbert Bay, at Tarbert, Argyll, Scotland, at the north end of Kintyre. Tarbert Castle was a strategic royal stronghold during the Middle Ages and one of three castles at Tarbert. The castle overlooks the harbour and although pre 14th century in construction, the tower dates back to 1494 and the visit of James IV to the Western Highlands.

Tarbert Castle today.

History

In 712, Tarbert was burned by King Selbach mac Ferchair of Cenél Loairn and of Dál Riata and in 731 by his son, Dúngal mac Selbaig.

King Edward II of England handed control of the castle to the Scottish King John II de Balliol in 1292. A fortified structure was built in Tarbert during the 13th century. It was reinforced with the addition of an outer bailey and towers in the 1320s by Robert the Bruce, to protect it against the Lords of the Isles. A towerhouse was added in the 16th century, which is the most noticeable part of the remains. The castle occupies high land above Loch Fyne, providing views up East Loch Tarbert and beyond to the Firth of Clyde. This castle was captured from John MacDonald of Islay, Lord of the Isles by James IV of Scotland as part of his campaign to destroy the power of the Lords of the Isles in 1494. In 1687 the castle was involved in another skirmish when Walter Campbell of Skipness Castle seized it as a stronghold for Archibald Campbell, 9th Earl of Argyll as part of actions in support of the Monmouth Rebellion in England.

There are only a couple of standing walls left and they are considered unstable. The castle has a very commanding view of the water approaches.

Constables of Tarbert Castle

- John de Lany 1326
- Charles MacAlister 1481

Bibliography

- David Hicks (1982), The Highland Clans, ISBN 9780091447403
- Annals of Ulster, AD 431-1201 (vols. 1 and 2) edition [1] and translation [2]

External websites

- Tarbert Royal Castle [3]

Geographical coordinates: 55°51′49″N 5°24′31″W

Torrisdale Castle

Torrisdale Castle

Torrisdale Castle is a historic mansion residence, overlooking Torrisdale Bay, south of Carradale, Kintyre, Scotland. The castle is situated at the edge of the village of Torrisdale.

History

The mansion was built in 1815, by General Keith Macalister, of Loup and Torrisdale in 1815. Designed by architect James Gillespie Graham, the mansion is castellated and consists of two storeys and a basement. Further extensions occurred in the 1900s.

The estate is home to the Macalister Hall family who have owned Torrisdale since 1890. A number of lodges, cottages, houses and even apartments within the mansion are available as tourist accommodation. An organic Tannery & Craft Shop also run on the estate.

External links

• Digital Images of Torrisdale Castle [1]

Geographical coordinates: 55°34′8″N 5°30′5″W

Kilberry Castle

Kilberry Castle

Kilberry Castle is a mansion house near the village of Kilberry, Knapdale, Argyll and Bute, Scotland. Built in 1497 as a castle, it was destroyed in 1513 and the remains were incorporated into a castellated mansion house built in 1844. Further additions occurred in 1871.

History

Originally built in 1497 as a L-plan castle by a cadet branch of Clan Campbell. The castle was destroyed by an English pirate in 1513. The remains of the old castle were incorporated into the mansion built in 1844 by John Campbell, with the mansion being enlarged in 1871.

References

Geographical coordinates: 55°48′58″N 5°39′45″W

Kilkerran Castle

Kilkerran Castle

Kilkerran Castle is a ruined castle, near Campbeltown, Kintyre, Argyll and Bute, Scotland.

History

A keep was built in 1490 by King James IV, for the housing of a garrison to subdue the MacDonalds.

Further fortification works were undertaken by King James V, during an expedition to the Isles in 1536 against the Macdonalds and other turbulent clans.

References

Geographical coordinates: 55°25′1″N 5°35′23″W

Askomill House

Askomill House

Askomill House

Island Muller, Kintyre, Scotland

Coordinates	55°26′12″N 5°32′20″W

Askomill House is a ruined fortified house on a promontory known as Isla Muller (or Island Muller), Kintyre, Argyll and Bute, Scotland, north of Campbeltown.

History

Askomill House was the home of Angus Macdonald, 8th of Dunnyveg. In 1598, the house was surrounded by his son, James MacDonald and between two or three hundred armed men with the house being set on fire and Angus being taken prisoner.

Faslane Castle, Shandon Castle, and St Michael's Chapel

Faslane Castle, Shandon Castle, and St Michael's Chapel

Faslane Castle and **Shandon Castle** were two mediaeval Scottish castles which once stood between the towns Garelochhead and Helensburgh, near the shores of the Gare Loch, in Argyll and Bute. In the 19th century, the castles were thought to have dated back to the Middle Ages. At that time period, they were situated in within the mormaerdom of Lennox, which was controlled by the mormaers of Lennox. Today nothing remains of Faslane Castle; though in the 19th century certain ruins of Shandon Castle were said to have still existed. Near the site of Faslane Castle sits the ruinous **St Michael's Chapel**, which has also been thought to date to the Middle Ages.

Faslane Castle

Faslane Castle (grid reference NS24949016) is a castle which once stood near Faslane, in Argyll and Bute (and also within the old county of Dunbartonshire). The site of the castle is located about 1.7 miles (3 km) north of the modern town of Shandon; and about 1 mile (2 km) south of the town of Garelochhead. The site sits overlooking the Gare Loch and is today dominated by the Her Majesty's Naval Base Clyde.

In the Middle Ages, the lands of Dunbartonshire were then part of the Lennox, and were controlled by the mormaers of Lennox. The early 13th century mormaer Ailín II granted an extensive tract of land lying on the eastern side of the Gare Loch to one of his younger sons, Amhlaíbh. Descending from Amhlaíbh was Walter of Faslane, who was the great-grandson of Ailín II. On the death of Mormaer Domhnall, Walter became the representative of the male line of the house of Lennox. With his marriage to Margaret, daughter of Domhnall, Walter became mormaer in his own right.

The castle, according to 19th century historian William Fraser, was said to have dated back to the 12th century. The 21st century mediaevalist Geoffrey Stell compiled a census of mottes within Scotland and listed only four in Dunbartonshire—one of which is Faslane. According to Fraser, the castle was often occupied by earls of Lennox, or members of their family.

> *Than to Faslan the worthy Scottis can pass,*
> *Quhar erll Malcom was bidand at defence;*
> *Rycht glaid he was off Wallace gud presence.*
>
> — Blind Harry, *The Wallace*

Faslane Castle makes an appearance in the 15th century epic poem, known as *The Wallace*, composed by the *maker* Blind Harry. The story runs that Wallace sacked the town of Dumbarton, and laid waste the castle of Rosneath—the modern village of Rosneath sits on the opposite side of the Gare Loch from the sites of Faslane, Shandon, and Ardincaple castles. He then proceeded across the loch to Faslane Castle, where he was warmly received by Mormaer Maol Choluim I.

In 1543, Faslane was bestowed by Matthew Stewart, Earl of Lennox on Adam Colquhoun. In 1567, it and Garelochhead were acquired by Campbell of Ardkinlass, who sold it before 1583 to Campbell of Carrick. In 1693 it was in the hands of Sir John Colquhoun of Luss, who feud it to Archibald MacAulay of Ardincaple. According to the 19th century historian Joseph Irving, in the mid 18th century the ruined Faslane Castle "furnished a shelter to the last representative of a once powerful family"—the last clan chief of the MacAulays of Ardincaple.

Fraser stated in 1869, that no buildings or any part of the castle was then visible. He stated that the only remaining trace of the castle was a green mound, which overlooked the junction of two deep glens, between two small rivulets of which the banks were steep. William Charles Maughan stated that the site of the castle could be distinguished, at the time of his writing, "by a small mound near the murmuring burn which flows into the bay". Maughan also wrote that at Faslane there stood an oak tree at place called in Scottish Gaelic *Cnoch-na-Cullah* (English: "knoll of the cock"); and that according to legend, when a cock crowed beneath the branches of the old oak upon the knoll, a member of Clan MacAulay was about to die.

It has been stated that the site of Faslane Castle was destroyed when the West Highland Railway was built over top of the site, in 1891–1894.

St Michael's Chapel

56°4'10"N 4°48'53"W

Near the site of the castle is St Michael's Chapel (grid reference NS2489589862). Fraser described the ruins of the chapel as measuring 43 by 23 feet (13.1 by 7.0 m). He stated that stones had been removed from the site, except for two gable ends that still stood at the time of his writing (1869). He wrote that the foundations of what was reputed to be the priest's house, could still be seen between the chapel and the barn. On the site he noted that on the site of the stream, located beneath the bank, there was a spring called "The Priest's Well". George Chalmers, and the late 19th and early 20th century architects David MacGibbon and Thomas Ross, stated that the chapel had apparently been dedicated to St Michael, and that it may date from the 13th or 14th century. In 1963, the OS visited the site and noted that the chapel and the south wall had

Ruinous St Michael's Chapel, about 1869.

been rebuilt (without mortar), to a height of 1.3 metres (4.3 ft). However, there were no traces of the original burying ground, the priest's house, or the well. The site is currently situated within a modern cemetery.

The website for St Michaels Roman Catholic Church, in Dumbarton, states that there is a tradition of dedicating churches to the saint within the area. For example, in Glen Luss, there are the remains of a pre-Reformation church dedicated to the saint; in Helensburgh there is an Episcopalian church named 'Saint Michael and the Angels'; and in the Middle Ages there once was a chapel dedicated to St Michael in the Strathleven area of Dumbarton.

Shandon Castle

56°3'6"N 4°47'59"W

Shandon Castle (grid reference NS257878) was a castle which once stood near the town of Shandon—the town is situated between site of Faslane and the town of Helensburgh, which is situated on the shores of the Gare Loch. Fraser described the site of Shandon Castle as being on a hillside, above the house of Shandon. Fraser stated that remains of the castle still existed at the time of his writing and that the site was called "the old Dun". According to Fraser, no traditions concerning the castle then existed.

See also

- Clan MacAulay, a Scottish clan which was once centred near the castle sites.
- Mormaer of Lennox, once lords of the Lennox district.

References

Geographical coordinates: 56°4′20″N 4°48′50″W

Sources

- Irving, Joseph (1879). *The Book of Dumbartonshire* [1]. **1**. Edinburgh: W. and A. K. Johnston.
- Irving, Joseph (1879). *The Book of Dumbartonshire* [2]. **2**. Edinburgh: W. and A. K. Johnston.
- Fraser, William (1869). *The Chiefs of Colquhoun and their Country* [3]. **2**. Edinburgh: T. & A. Constable.
- Liddiard, Robert, ed (2003). *Anglo-Norman Castles*. Woodbridge: The Boydell Press. ISBN 0 85115 904 4.
- Maughan, William Charles (1897). *Annals of Garelochside, being an account historical and topographical of the parishes of Row, Rosneath and Cardross* [4]. Paisley: A. Gardner.
- Moir, James, ed (1889). *The Actis and Deidis of the Illustere and Vailyeand Campioun Schir William Wallace, Knicht of Ellerslie* [5]. Edinburgh: William Blackwood and Sons.

Stonefield Castle

Stonefield Castle

Stonefield Castle, also known as *Barmore House*, is a Scottish baronial manor house near the village of Stonefield, north of Tarbert, Knapdale, Argyll & Bute, Scotland.

Built in 1837 and designed by architects William Henry Playfair and William Notman.

References

Geographical coordinates: 55°53′29″N 5°24′58″W

Airds Castle

Airds Castle

Airds Castle is a ruined castle near Carradale, Kintyre, Argyll and Bute, Scotland. The castle held a position on the summit of a rock outcrop between Carradale harbour and the bay of Port Righ.

History

King James IV of Scotland, fortified the castle of Ardcardle (Airds) in c1490's.

References

- McKerral, Andrew (1948). *Kintyre in the 17th Century.*
- "Airds Castle" [1]. 2009. Retrieved 2009-08-03.

Geographical coordinates: 55°35′22″N 5°27′42″W

Auchenbreck Castle

Auchenbreck Castle

Auchenbreck Castle (or **Auchinbreck**) is located in Argyll, Scotland. Its remains are situated in Kilmodan parish, near the mouth of Glendaruel, 9 kilometres (5.6 mi) north of Tighnabruaich on the Cowal peninsula. Little remains of the castle, other than a flat rectangular platform, around 35 by 18 metres (115 by 59 ft), between Auchenbreck farmhouse and the Auchenbreck Burn. This is partially bounded by a revetment wall up to 2.2 metres (7 ft 3 in) high.

The castle was held by the Campbells of Auchinbreck, a branch of the Clan Campbell descended from Duncan, a younger son of Duncan Campbell, 1st Lord Campbell. He was granted lands near Dunoon in 1435, and further lands in Glassary. By the 16th century, the family were known as "of Auchinbreck", and the castle appears on Timothy Pont's map of the late 16th century. Around 1703 the castle was purchased by John Fullarton, former minister of Kilmodan, and later Bishop of Edinburgh. Fullarton renamed the estate Greenhall, and was the last person to live in the castle. When the estate was sold in 1728, after Fullarton's death, it included a mansion which may have been built from the stones of the castle. The castle itself was in its current ruined state by 1870.

External links

- "Auchenbreck Castle, Site Number NS08SW 1" [1]. *CANMORE*. RCAHMS. Retrieved 2009-09-14.

Geographical coordinates: 55°59′06″N 5°10′34″W

Saddell Castle

Saddell Castle

Saddell Castle is a 16th century tower house on the shore of the Kilbrannan Sound near Saddell, Kintyre, Argyll and Bute, Scotland.

History

Built by David Hamilton, Bishop of Argyll, between 1508–1512, the castle was built from the stones of the ruined Saddell Abbey. The castle was gifted to James Hamilton, 2nd Earl of Arran by Bishop James Hamilton, as payment of debts and taxes in 1556. The Earl of Arran exchanged it with the Chief of Clan MacDonald of Dunnyveg, James MacDonald in exchange for James's lands on the Isle of Arran. The castle was ransacked and burnt in 1558 by Thomas

Saddell Castle by the Saddell Water

Radclyffe, 3rd Earl of Sussex, Lord Deputy of Ireland under orders of Queen Mary I of England in retaliation of James's involvement in Ireland against the English. The castle was later rebuilt and enlarged together with a trap door in the main entrance passage, which upon activation, sent unwanted visitors into a dungeon which had no exits. In 1607, the Clan Donald lands in Kintyre, including Saddell, were conveyed by King James VI to Archibald Campbell, 7th Earl of Argyll. The castle fell into disrepair when Saddell House was built c.1774. The castle was bought by the Landmark Trust and the castle was restored. The castle can be rented out as a self-catering property from the Landmark Trust.

References

- "Saddell Castle" [1]. *The Chatelaine's Scottish Castles*. Retrieved 2009-09-22.
- Rev. James Webb. "Saddell Castle" [2]. *Ralston Genealogy*. Retrieved 2009-09-22.

Geographical coordinates: 55°31′38″N 5°30′17″W

Loch Gorm Castle

Loch Gorm Castle

Loch Gorm Castle is a ruined castle located on the isle of Eilean Mór on Loch Gorm, Islay, Scotland. It was once a stronghold of Clan Macdonald.

The castle was square, with a round bastion at each corner. The castle was occupied temporarily by Sir Lachlan Mor Maclean of Duart who was besieged in 1578 by the MacDonalds with the assistance of the Colin Campbell, 6th Earl of Argyll. Ruinous from 1586, royal forces led by Andrew Stuart, 3rd Lord Ochiltree demolished the castle in 1608. Sir James MacDonald retook the island in April 1615 and left a garrison upon Eilean Mór. A private garrison was maintained upon Eilean Mór between 1639-40.

References

- Islay Info Blog [1]
- Site Record - Loch Gorm Castle - The Royal Commission on the Ancient and Historical Monuments of Scotland [2]

Geographical coordinates: 55°48′12″N 6°24′51″W

Largie Castle, Tayinloan

Largie Castle, Tayinloan

Largie Castle is a former mansion house at Tayinloan, Argyll and Bute, Scotland. The house was designed by architect Charles Wilson and was built in 1857-9. The house was pulled down in 1958.

References

Geographical coordinates: 55°39′19.52″N 5°38′56.25″W

Largie Castle, Rhunahaorine

Largie Castle, Rhunahaorine

Largie Castle is a ruined castle at Rhunahaorine, Argyll and Bute, Scotland.

History

The castle was built by Clan MacDonald of Largie.

After the battle of Rhunahaorine Moss, the castle was razed by the forces of General David Leslie in 1647.

References

Geographical coordinates: 55°40′28″N 5°38′40″W

Cairnburgh Castle

Cairnburgh Castle

Cairnburgh Castle is a ruined castle that is located on the islands of Cairn na Burgh Mòr and Cairn na Burgh Beag, Argyll and Bute, Scotland. These islands are at the northern extremity of the Treshnish Isles at the mouth of Loch Tuath, Mull north of Iona. 1991's *The Changing Scottish Landscape* characterizes it as "one of the most isolated fortifications in Britain...[and] also one of the strangest."

Structure

An unusual feature of the castle its that its defences straddle both islands. Cairn na Burgh Mòr contains a barrack block, chapel, courtyard and guard-house and its smaller companion isle has another guard-house and a well.

History

The castle, which may have begun its existence as a Viking fortress called Kiarnaborg, has been held by a variety of individuals since its first recorded appearance in 1249. It is mentioned in the 13th century *Hákonar saga Hákonarsonar* as the property of an island king of the family of Somerled, demanded of him by Alexander III of Scotland. The *Gazetteer for Scotland* reports that the castle's owner at least from 1249 to 1269 was Clan MacDougall, descendants of Somerled through his son Dubgall. When the MacDougall clan supported John de Balliol against Robert de Brus in the Wars of Scottish Independence, the Crown seized the castle. Temporarily occupied by Clan MacDonald, it at some point became the property of Clan MacLean.

While the property of the MacLeans, the castle was the location of several conflicts, but it was extremely well defended by the cliffs that surrounded it. It was besieged in 1504 by James IV when the MacLeans rebelled. It was briefly taken in 1647 during the War of the Three Kingdoms by General David Leslie. In the next decade, it was torched by Oliver Cromwell's New Model Army. The fire likely caused the demise of a number of manuscripts that had been conveyed to the castle for safety from Iona after the 1561 Act calling for the destruction of "Monuments of Idolatry". In 1679, it stood against the Campbells, but did not stand when attacked again in 1692.

Twice during the Jacobite Risings, in 1715 and 1745, the government used Cairnsburgh to house troops. In 1759 it was the birthplace of author Isabella Kelly.

References

- Cairn na burgh beg [1]
- Cairn na burgh more [2]
- Cairnburgh Castle [3]
- Corcoran, James Andrew; Patrick John Ryan; Edmond Francis Prendergast (1902). *The American Catholic quarterly review* [4]. Hardy and Mahony.. Retrieved 6 June 2010.
- Marsden, John (1 January 2010). *Somerled: And the Emergence of Gaelic Scotland* [5]. Tuckwell Press, Ltd.. ISBN 9781904607809. Retrieved 6 June 2010.
- Skene, William F. (1876). *Celtic Scotland: a history of ancient Alban* [6]. Edmonston & Douglas. Retrieved 6 June 2010.
- Stewart, William; Steven Barfield (July 2007). *British and Irish poets: a biographical dictionary, 449-2006* [7]. McFarland. ISBN 9780786428915. Retrieved 6 June 2010.
- Whyte, Ian D.; Kathleen A. Whyte (1991). *The changing Scottish landscape, 1500-1800* [8]. Taylor & Francis. pp. 91–. ISBN 9780415029926. Retrieved 6 June 2010.
- Whyte, Ian D.; Kathleen A. Whyte (1990). *On the trail of the Jacobites* [9]. Taylor & Francis. ISBN 9780415033343. Retrieved 6 June 2010.

Notes

Geographical coordinates: 56°31′6″N 6°22′52″W

Glengorm Castle

Glengorm Castle

Glengorm Castle	
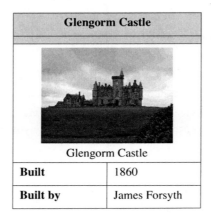 Glengorm Castle	
Built	1860
Built by	James Forsyth

Glengorm Castle is a 19th century castle on the Isle of Mull near Tobermory. The castle is located on a headland and overlooks the Atlantic Ocean. On a clear day the Outer Hebrides and Islands of Uist, Rùm and Canna can be viewed from the castle.

The castle was built in 1860 for James Forsyth.

References

- "Glengorm Castle" [1]. CANMORE. Retrieved 3 July 2010.

Geographical coordinates: 56°38′12.6″N 6°10′38.42″W

Calgary Castle

Calgary Castle

Calgary Castle	
Built	1823
Built by	Alan MacAskill

Calgary Castle, also known as *Calgary House*, is a 19th century castellated gothic mansion at Calgary on the Isle of Mull, Scotland. The mansion house was built in 1817 by Captain Alan MacAskill.

Calgary Castle was owned by Col. Eric and Elizabeth Mackenzie from 1948 until the 1970's who planted over 150 species of rhododendron and exotic plants and created the woodland garden which is still famous today.

References

- "Calgary Castle". CANMORE.

Geographical coordinates: 56°34′50.17″N 6°16′13.9″W

Barcaldine Castle

Barcaldine Castle

Barcaldine Castle	
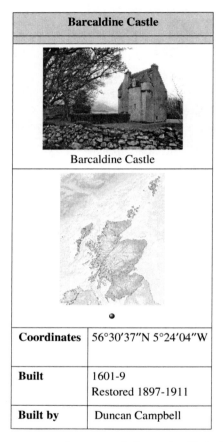 Barcaldine Castle	
Coordinates	56°30′37″N 5°24′04″W
Built	1601-9 Restored 1897-1911
Built by	Duncan Campbell

Barcaldine Castle is a 17th century tower house castle located at Barcaldine near Oban, Scotland. The castle was built by Sir Duncan Campbell, of Glenorchy, between 1601 and 1609. The castle fell into desrepair in the later 19th century, when Barcaldine House became the principle residence of the family. It was restored between 1897-1911 and now operates as a hotel.

References

- [[CANMORE [1]] Royal Commission on the Ancient and Historical Monuments of Scotland listing - Barcaldine Castle]
- Barcaldine Castle website [2]

Aros Castle

Aros Castle

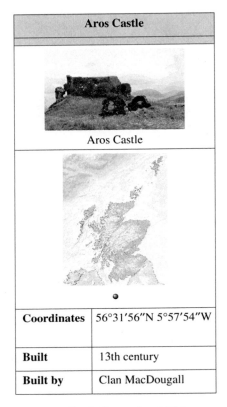

Aros Castle	
Aros Castle	
Coordinates	56°31′56″N 5°57′54″W
Built	13th century
Built by	Clan MacDougall

Aros Castle, also known as *Dounarwyse Castle*, is a ruined 13th century castle near Salenn on the Isle of Mull, Scotland. The castle overlooks the Sound of Mull.

The castle was a stronghold of the Clan MacDougall, Clan Donald and Clan Maclean during its occupation.

References

- [[CANMORE [1]] Royal Commission on the Ancient and Historical Monuments of Scotland listing - Aros Castle]

Fincharn Castle

Fincharn Castle

Fincharn Castle	
Built	13th century
Built by	Lord of Glassary

Fincharn Castle, also known as *Fionchairn Castle* and *Glassery Castle*, is a ruined 13th century castle near Ford on the southwest shore of Loch Awe, Scotland. The castle was built in 1240 by the Lord of Glassary.

References

- "Fincharn Castle" [1]. CANMORE. Retrieved 3 July 2010.

Geographical coordinates: 56°11′10.21″N 5°23′17″W

Innes Chonnel Castle

Innes Chonnel Castle

Innes Chonnel Castle	
Innes Chonnel Castle	
Coordinates	56°15′23″N 5°16′09″W
Built	13th century

Innes Chonnel Castle is a ruined 13th century castle on a island on Loch Awe near Dalavich, Scotland. It was once a stronghold of Clan Campbell.

References

- [[CANMORE [1]] Royal Commission on the Ancient and Historical Monuments of Scotland listing - Innes Chonnel Castle]

Kilmartin Castle

Kilmartin Castle

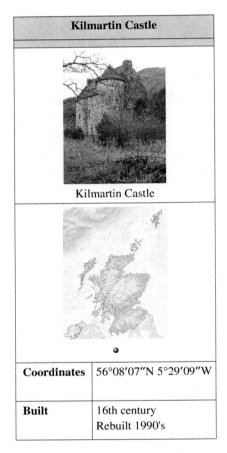

Kilmartin Castle	
Kilmartin Castle	
Coordinates	56°08′07″N 5°29′09″W
Built	16th century
Rebuilt 1990's

Kilmartin Castle is a 16th century Z-plan tower house castle at Kilmartin, Scotland. Built by the Rector of Kilmartin and later owned by Clan Campbell.

Reference

- [[CANMORE [1]] Royal Commission on the Ancient and Historical Monuments of Scotland listing - Kilmartin Castle]

Lachlan Castle

Lachlan Castle

Lachlan Castle	
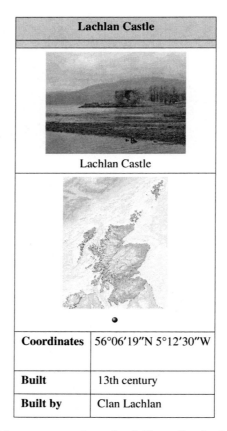 Lachlan Castle	
Coordinates	56°06′19″N 5°12′30″W
Built	13th century
Built by	Clan Lachlan

Lachlan Castle is a ruined 13th century castle on Loch Fyne, Scotland. It was the stronghold of Clan Lachlan.

References

- [[CANMORE [1]] Royal Commission on the Ancient and Historical Monuments of Scotland listing - Lachlan Castle]

Minard Castle

Minard Castle

Minard Castle	
Built	19th century

Minard Castle is a 19th century casellated mansion on the north-western shore of Loch Fyne, Scotland.

References

- "Minard Castle" [1]. CANMORE. Retrieved 3 July 2010.

Geographical coordinates: 56°5′52.53″N 5°15′34.81″W

Breachacha Castle

Breachacha Castle

Breachacha Castle is a 14th-15th century tower house castle at Breachacha, Coll, Scotland. It was a stronghold of the MacLeans of Coll and overlooks Loch Breachacha. The castle fell in ruin in the late eighteenth century and was restored in the 20th century by Major N V MacLean Bristol.

References

- "Breachacha Castle" [1]. CANMORE. Retrieved 3 July 2010.
- Gaelic Rings - Coll [2]

Geographical coordinates: 56°35′28″N 6°37′43″W

Article Sources and Contributors

Inveraray Castle *Source*: http://en.wikipedia.org/?oldid=387227795 *Contributors*:

Kilchurn Castle *Source*: http://en.wikipedia.org/?oldid=380851039 *Contributors*: Hmains

Duart Castle *Source*: http://en.wikipedia.org/?oldid=366546530 *Contributors*: Jllm06

Castle Stalker *Source*: http://en.wikipedia.org/?oldid=390356724 *Contributors*: JustAGal

Dunollie Castle *Source*: http://en.wikipedia.org/?oldid=371168816 *Contributors*: Ben MacDui

Kilmory Castle *Source*: http://en.wikipedia.org/?oldid=301304907 *Contributors*: 1 anonymous edits

Gylen Castle *Source*: http://en.wikipedia.org/?oldid=285677599 *Contributors*: Jonathan Oldenbuck

Dunstaffnage Castle *Source*: http://en.wikipedia.org/?oldid=387614811 *Contributors*: 1 anonymous edits

Duntrune Castle *Source*: http://en.wikipedia.org/?oldid=380384460 *Contributors*: Chemical Engineer

Dunans Castle *Source*: http://en.wikipedia.org/?oldid=353110169 *Contributors*: 1 anonymous edits

Carnasserie Castle *Source*: http://en.wikipedia.org/?oldid=363623479 *Contributors*: 1 anonymous edits

Skipness Castle *Source*: http://en.wikipedia.org/?oldid=379429688 *Contributors*: Mild Bill Hiccup

Claig Castle *Source*: http://en.wikipedia.org/?oldid=304298256 *Contributors*: Finavon

Dunaverty Castle *Source*: http://en.wikipedia.org/?oldid=384914122 *Contributors*: 1 anonymous edits

Castle Toward *Source*: http://en.wikipedia.org/?oldid=367866188 *Contributors*: JForget

Torosay Castle *Source*: http://en.wikipedia.org/?oldid=375058139 *Contributors*: 1 anonymous edits

Coeffin *Source*: http://en.wikipedia.org/?oldid=372590358 *Contributors*: Colonies Chris

Castle Sween *Source*: http://en.wikipedia.org/?oldid=368877627 *Contributors*: 1 anonymous edits

Achallader Castle *Source*: http://en.wikipedia.org/?oldid=388241048 *Contributors*: 1 anonymous edits

Rothesay Castle *Source*: http://en.wikipedia.org/?oldid=339307443 *Contributors*:

Dunderave Castle *Source*: http://en.wikipedia.org/?oldid=383621476 *Contributors*: Jonathan Oldenbuck

Kilmahew Castle *Source*: http://en.wikipedia.org/?oldid=355546196 *Contributors*: LeeNapier

Kames Castle *Source*: http://en.wikipedia.org/?oldid=304352641 *Contributors*: Finavon

Tullichewan *Source*: http://en.wikipedia.org/?oldid=364291569 *Contributors*: Butterboy

Dunyvaig Castle *Source*: http://en.wikipedia.org/?oldid=334203563 *Contributors*:

Ardencaple Castle *Source*: http://en.wikipedia.org/?oldid=348115418 *Contributors*: Mais oui!

Achanduin Castle *Source*: http://en.wikipedia.org/?oldid=381290023 *Contributors*: Jalo

Finlaggan *Source*: http://en.wikipedia.org/?oldid=358456807 *Contributors*: Ben MacDui

Finlaggan Castle *Source*: http://en.wikipedia.org/?oldid=384459079 *Contributors*:

Carrick Castle *Source*: http://en.wikipedia.org/?oldid=383621561 *Contributors*: Jonathan Oldenbuck

Craignish Castle *Source*: http://en.wikipedia.org/?oldid=304299922 *Contributors*: Finavon

Moy Castle *Source*: http://en.wikipedia.org/?oldid=380230593 *Contributors*: Hmains

Tarbert Castle *Source*: http://en.wikipedia.org/?oldid=378344352 *Contributors*: Woohookitty

Torrisdale Castle *Source*: http://en.wikipedia.org/?oldid=351538410 *Contributors*: Mais oui!

Kilberry Castle *Source*: http://en.wikipedia.org/?oldid=304302457 *Contributors*: Finavon

Kilkerran Castle *Source*: http://en.wikipedia.org/?oldid=304426297 *Contributors*: Newm30

Askomill House *Source*: http://en.wikipedia.org/?oldid=365956993 *Contributors*: Newm30

Faslane Castle, Shandon Castle, and St Michael's Chapel *Source*: http://en.wikipedia.org/?oldid=354709988 *Contributors*: 1 anonymous edits

Stonefield Castle *Source*: http://en.wikipedia.org/?oldid=306297725 *Contributors*: Finavon

Airds Castle *Source*: http://en.wikipedia.org/?oldid=306103550 *Contributors*: Finavon

Auchenbreck Castle *Source*: http://en.wikipedia.org/?oldid=313806046 *Contributors*: Jonathan Oldenbuck

Saddell Castle *Source*: http://en.wikipedia.org/?oldid=383621911 *Contributors*: Jonathan Oldenbuck

Loch Gorm Castle *Source*: http://en.wikipedia.org/?oldid=386879500 *Contributors*:

Largie Castle, Tayinloan *Source*: http://en.wikipedia.org/?oldid=371600312 *Contributors*: Finavon

Largie Castle, Rhunahaorine *Source*: http://en.wikipedia.org/?oldid=371599917 *Contributors*: Finavon

Cairnburgh Castle *Source*: http://en.wikipedia.org/?oldid=371594897 *Contributors*: Finavon

Glengorm Castle *Source*: http://en.wikipedia.org/?oldid=371596139 *Contributors*: Finavon

Calgary Castle *Source*: http://en.wikipedia.org/?oldid=388369541 *Contributors*: 1 anonymous edits

Barcaldine Castle *Source*: http://en.wikipedia.org/?oldid=383621348 *Contributors*: Jonathan Oldenbuck

Aros Castle *Source*: http://en.wikipedia.org/?oldid=366310790 *Contributors*: Newm30

Fincharn Castle *Source*: http://en.wikipedia.org/?oldid=371595408 *Contributors*: Finavon

Innes Chonnel Castle *Source*: http://en.wikipedia.org/?oldid=366328250 *Contributors*: Newm30

Kilmartin Castle *Source*: http://en.wikipedia.org/?oldid=366329628 *Contributors*: Newm30

Lachlan Castle *Source*: http://en.wikipedia.org/?oldid=366331252 *Contributors*: Newm30

Minard Castle *Source*: http://en.wikipedia.org/?oldid=371597152 *Contributors*: Finavon

Breachacha Castle *Source*: http://en.wikipedia.org/?oldid=371594172 *Contributors*: Finavon

Image Sources, Licenses and Contributors

File:Inverary Castle Morris edited.jpg *Source*: http://en.wikipedia.org/w/index.php?title=File:Inverary_Castle_Morris_edited.jpg *License*: Public Domain *Contributors*: Chicheley, Merchbow, Mmxx, 3 anonymous edits

File:Inveraray Castle from above.jpg *Source*: http://en.wikipedia.org/w/index.php?title=File:Inveraray_Castle_from_above.jpg *License*: Creative Commons Attribution 2.5 *Contributors*: StaraBlazkova

File:Kilchurn Castle from the boat.jpg *Source*: http://en.wikipedia.org/w/index.php?title=File:Kilchurn_Castle_from_the_boat.jpg *License*: unknown *Contributors*: Peter Gordon

File:Kilchurn Castle engraving by William Miller after H McCulloch.jpg *Source*: http://en.wikipedia.org/w/index.php?title=File:Kilchurn_Castle_engraving_by_William_Miller_after_H_McCulloch.jpg *License*: Public Domain *Contributors*: William Miller

Image:Duart Castle.jpg *Source*: http://en.wikipedia.org/w/index.php?title=File:Duart_Castle.jpg *License*: Public Domain *Contributors*: Jonathan Oldenbuck, 汲平, 1 anonymous edits

Image:TyDuartCastle20030825r20f02.jpg *Source*: http://en.wikipedia.org/w/index.php?title=File:TyDuartCastle20030825r20f02.jpg *License*: Public Domain *Contributors*: User:DrTorstenHenning

File:Castle_stalker2.jpg *Source*: http://en.wikipedia.org/w/index.php?title=File:Castle_stalker2.jpg *License*: Creative Commons Attribution-Sharealike 3.0 *Contributors*: User:Gil.cavalcanti

Image:Castle_Stalker_01.jpg *Source*: http://en.wikipedia.org/w/index.php?title=File:Castle_Stalker_01.jpg *License*: Creative Commons Attribution 2.0 *Contributors*: Gustavo Naharro from Valencia, Spain

Image:Castle_Stalker_-_geograph.org.uk_-_7001.jpg *Source*: http://en.wikipedia.org/w/index.php?title=File:Castle_Stalker_-_geograph.org.uk_-_7001.jpg *License*: unknown *Contributors*: Kilom691, Podzemnik

Image:Scotlandcastlestalker.jpg *Source*: http://en.wikipedia.org/w/index.php?title=File:Scotlandcastlestalker.jpg *License*: Creative Commons Attribution-Sharealike 2.0 *Contributors*: Chrys

Image:DUNOLLIE_Castle_Front.JPG *Source*: http://en.wikipedia.org/w/index.php?title=File:DUNOLLIE_Castle_Front.JPG *License*: GNU Free Documentation License *Contributors*: Jjhake, Ranveig

Image:KilmoryCastle(PatrickMackie)May2006.jpg *Source*: http://en.wikipedia.org/w/index.php?title=File:KilmoryCastle(PatrickMackie)May2006.jpg *License*: unknown *Contributors*: Akinom, Edward, Liftarn

Image:Kilmory Castle Location.png *Source*: http://en.wikipedia.org/w/index.php?title=File:Kilmory_Castle_Location.png *License*: GNU Free Documentation License *Contributors*: Akinom, Supergolden

Image:Gylen castle isle of kerrera scotland by day.JPG *Source*: http://en.wikipedia.org/w/index.php?title=File:Gylen_castle_isle_of_kerrera_scotland_by_day.JPG *License*: Public Domain *Contributors*: Original uploader was Jimieee at en.wikipedia

Image:Dunstaffnage Castle.jpg *Source*: http://en.wikipedia.org/w/index.php?title=File:Dunstaffnage_Castle.jpg *License*: unknown *Contributors*: Asta, Cactus.man, Crosbiesmith, Eusebius, JeremyA, Kurpfalzbilder.de

File:Scotland relief location map.jpg *Source*: http://en.wikipedia.org/w/index.php?title=File:Scotland_relief_location_map.jpg *License*: GNU Free Documentation License *Contributors*: User:NordNordWest, User:Uwe Dedering

File:Red_pog.svg *Source*: http://en.wikipedia.org/w/index.php?title=File:Red_pog.svg *License*: Public Domain *Contributors*: User:Andux

Image:Dunstaffnage01.jpg *Source*: http://en.wikipedia.org/w/index.php?title=File:Dunstaffnage01.jpg *License*: Creative Commons Attribution-Sharealike 2.5 *Contributors*: User:Supergolden

Image:Dunstaffnage Castle plan.png *Source*: http://en.wikipedia.org/w/index.php?title=File:Dunstaffnage_Castle_plan.png *License*: Creative Commons Attribution-Sharealike 3.0 *Contributors*: User:Jonathan Oldenbuck

Image:Dunstaffnage02.jpg *Source*: http://en.wikipedia.org/w/index.php?title=File:Dunstaffnage02.jpg *License*: Creative Commons Attribution-Sharealike 2.5 *Contributors*: User:Supergolden

Image:Dunstaffnage03.jpg *Source*: http://en.wikipedia.org/w/index.php?title=File:Dunstaffnage03.jpg *License*: Creative Commons Attribution-Sharealike 2.5 *Contributors*: User:Supergolden

Image:DunstaffnageChapel.jpg *Source*: http://en.wikipedia.org/w/index.php?title=File:DunstaffnageChapel.jpg *License*: Creative Commons Attribution-Sharealike 2.5 *Contributors*: User:Supergolden

Image:DuntruneCastle(PatrickMackie)Jun2006.jpg *Source*: http://en.wikipedia.org/w/index.php?title=File:DuntruneCastle(PatrickMackie)Jun2006.jpg *License*: unknown *Contributors*: Akinom, Edward, Liftarn

Image:Duntrune Castle Location.png *Source*: http://en.wikipedia.org/w/index.php?title=File:Duntrune_Castle_Location.png *License*: GNU Free Documentation License *Contributors*: Supergolden, 1 anonymous edits

Image:Dunans castle.jpg *Source*: http://en.wikipedia.org/w/index.php?title=File:Dunans_castle.jpg *License*: Public Domain *Contributors*: Original uploader was Slink pink at en.wikipedia

Image:Dunans castle bridge.jpg *Source*: http://en.wikipedia.org/w/index.php?title=File:Dunans_castle_bridge.jpg *License*: Public Domain *Contributors*: Original uploader was Slink pink at en.wikipedia

Image:CarnasserieCastle001.jpg *Source*: http://en.wikipedia.org/w/index.php?title=File:CarnasserieCastle001.jpg *License*: unknown *Contributors*: Original uploader was Tumulus at en.wikipedia

Image:CarnasserieCastle002.jpg *Source*: http://en.wikipedia.org/w/index.php?title=File:CarnasserieCastle002.jpg *License*: unknown *Contributors*: Original uploader was Tumulus at en.wikipedia

File:Skipness Castle 20080425 from north west.jpg *Source*: http://en.wikipedia.org/w/index.php?title=File:Skipness_Castle_20080425_from_north_west.jpg *License*: GNU Free Documentation License *Contributors*: User:Otter

File:Castle Toward.jpg *Source*: http://en.wikipedia.org/w/index.php?title=File:Castle_Toward.jpg *License*: Attribution *Contributors*: william craig

File:Old Castle Toward.jpg *Source*: http://en.wikipedia.org/w/index.php?title=File:Old_Castle_Toward.jpg *License*: Attribution *Contributors*: John Ferguson

Image:Torosay Castle 01.jpg *Source*: http://en.wikipedia.org/w/index.php?title=File:Torosay_Castle_01.jpg *License*: unknown *Contributors*: Rob Farrow

Image:CastleCoeffinLismore-ARuinedMacDougallStronghold(ColinSmith)Aug1995.jpg *Source*: http://en.wikipedia.org/w/index.php?title=File:CastleCoeffinLismore-ARuinedMacDougallStronghold(ColinSmith)Aug1995.jpg *License*: Attribution *Contributors*: Colin Smith

File:Castlesween.jpg *Source*: http://en.wikipedia.org/w/index.php?title=File:Castlesween.jpg *License*: Creative Commons Attribution-Sharealike 2.5 *Contributors*: Original uploader was Malcam2 at en.wikipedia

Image:RothesayCastleNW.JPG *Source*: http://en.wikipedia.org/w/index.php?title=File:RothesayCastleNW.JPG *License*: Creative Commons Attribution 2.5 *Contributors*: User:Supergolden

Image:RothesayCastleS.jpg *Source*: http://en.wikipedia.org/w/index.php?title=File:RothesayCastleS.jpg *License*: GNU Free Documentation License *Contributors*: User:Supergolden

File:Dunderave Castle, Loch Fyne, Argyll - geograph.org.uk - 47961.jpg *Source*: http://en.wikipedia.org/w/index.php?title=File:Dunderave_Castle,_Loch_Fyne,_Argyll_-_geograph.org.uk_-_47961.jpg *License*: unknown *Contributors*: AnRo0002, Podzemnik

Image:Kilmahew.jpg *Source*: http://en.wikipedia.org/w/index.php?title=File:Kilmahew.jpg *License*: Public Domain *Contributors*: Original uploader was LeeNapier at en.wikipedia

Image:Kames Castle.jpg *Source*: http://en.wikipedia.org/w/index.php?title=File:Kames_Castle.jpg *License*: Attribution *Contributors*: Richard Dear

Image:Ardencaple Castle 1901.jpg *Source*: http://en.wikipedia.org/w/index.php?title=File:Ardencaple_Castle_1901.jpg *License*: Public Domain *Contributors*: Akinom, Cactus.man

Image:Sketch of an addition to Ardincaple Castle, by Robert Adam.jpg *Source*: http://en.wikipedia.org/w/index.php?title=File:Sketch_of_an_addition_to_Ardincaple_Castle,_by_Robert_Adam.jpg *License*: Public Domain *Contributors*: The original sketch was drawn by Robert Adam (1728–1792).

Image:ArdencapleCastle.jpg *Source*: http://en.wikipedia.org/w/index.php?title=File:ArdencapleCastle.jpg *License*: Creative Commons Attribution-Sharealike 2.5 *Contributors*: Original uploader was Stephen Mackenzie at en.wikipedia (Original text : Stephen Mackenzie (no institution))

File:Blue_pog.svg *Source*: http://en.wikipedia.org/w/index.php?title=File:Blue_pog.svg *License*: Public Domain *Contributors*: Andux, Antonsusi, Droll, Juiced lemon, STyx, TwoWings, WikipediaMaster, 6 anonymous edits

Image:Achadun Castle.jpg *Source*: http://en.wikipedia.org/w/index.php?title=File:Achadun_Castle.jpg *License*: Attribution *Contributors*: Paul Biggin

Image:Islands of Loch Finlaggan.jpg *Source*: http://en.wikipedia.org/w/index.php?title=File:Islands_of_Loch_Finlaggan.jpg *License*: unknown *Contributors*: Mick Garratt

Image:Carrick Castle.jpg *Source*: http://en.wikipedia.org/w/index.php?title=File:Carrick_Castle.jpg *License*: unknown *Contributors*: Gordon McKinlay

Image:Craignish.jpg *Source*: http://en.wikipedia.org/w/index.php?title=File:Craignish.jpg *License*: Public Domain *Contributors*: User:Habsburger

Image:Craignish-old.jpg *Source*: http://en.wikipedia.org/w/index.php?title=File:Craignish-old.jpg *License*: Public Domain *Contributors*: User:Habsburger

Image:Lochbuie House and Moy Castle.jpg *Source*: http://en.wikipedia.org/w/index.php?title=File:Lochbuie_House_and_Moy_Castle.jpg *License*: Attribution *Contributors*: Dave Fergusson

File:Tarbert Castle.jpg *Source*: http://en.wikipedia.org/w/index.php?title=File:Tarbert_Castle.jpg *License*: unknown *Contributors*: Chris Downer

File:Island Muller by Kilchousland. - geograph.org.uk - 86280.jpg *Source*: http://en.wikipedia.org/w/index.php?title=File:Island_Muller_by_Kilchousland._-_geograph.org.uk_-_86280.jpg *License*: unknown *Contributors*:

File:Ruinous Faslane Chapel.jpg *Source*: http://en.wikipedia.org/w/index.php?title=File:Ruinous_Faslane_Chapel.jpg *License*: Public Domain *Contributors*: unknown (not attributed).

File:Saddell Castle (2).jpg *Source*: http://en.wikipedia.org/w/index.php?title=File:Saddell_Castle_(2).jpg *License*: Attribution *Contributors*: Steve Partridge

File:Glengorm Castle - geograph.org.uk - 270415.jpg *Source*: http://en.wikipedia.org/w/index.php?title=File:Glengorm_Castle_-_geograph.org.uk_-_270415.jpg *License*: Attribution *Contributors*: Rob Farrow

File:Barcaldine Castle - geograph.org.uk - 346164.jpg *Source*: http://en.wikipedia.org/w/index.php?title=File:Barcaldine_Castle_-_geograph.org.uk_-_346164.jpg *License*: Attribution *Contributors*: Mike and Kirsty Grundy

File:Aros Castle - exterior.jpg *Source*: http://en.wikipedia.org/w/index.php?title=File:Aros_Castle_-_exterior.jpg *License*: GNU Free Documentation License *Contributors*: User:Otter

File:Innis Chonnell, Loch Awe, Argyll.jpg *Source*: http://en.wikipedia.org/w/index.php?title=File:Innis_Chonnell,_Loch_Awe,_Argyll.jpg *License*: Attribution *Contributors*: Brian D Osborne

File:Kilmartin Castle.jpg *Source*: http://en.wikipedia.org/w/index.php?title=File:Kilmartin_Castle.jpg *License*: Attribution *Contributors*: Patrick Mackie

File:Old Castle Lachlan.jpg *Source*: http://en.wikipedia.org/w/index.php?title=File:Old_Castle_Lachlan.jpg *License*: unknown *Contributors*: Akinom, AnRo0002, Celtus, Jonathan Oldenbuck, 1 anonymous edits

CPSIA information can be obtained at www.ICGtesting.com
Printed in the USA
BVOW061809161111

276286BV00003B/45/P